PELICAN BOOKS

PROGRESS, COEXISTENCE AND INTELLECTUAL FREEDOM

Andrei Dmitriyevich Sakharov was born in 1921. He was exempted from army service because of his academic brilliance, and in 1942, after graduating from Moscow University with honours in physics, he joined Dr Igor Y. Tamm at the Lebedev Institute. Working under Tamm, Sakharov gained his doctorate in cosmic ray research when he was twenty-six. Between 1948 and 1953, when he was elected to the Soviet Academy of Sciences, he contributed more than anyone to the development of the Russian H-bomb. From 1948 until 1957 his name disappeared from the public for security reasons, but in 1958, at a time when the Soviet atmosphere had begun to ease, he publicly criticized Soviet education reforms. In the early sixties he emerged as a critic of Soviet eclectic genetics, thus committing himself to the liberal and progressive side of an old and dangerous politico-scientific conflict. From 1965 his name began to appear more often, and in 1966 he and twenty-four other intellectuals signed a letter denouncing any attempt to rehabilitate Stalin. He was dismissed from his post as chief consultant to the State Committee on Atomic Energy in March 1969. Since 1970 he has been in the forefront of the movement for Human Rights in Russia, giving many interviews to foreign journalists despite increasing pressure from the K.G.B. In 1975 he published a book in Britain (though not in Russia) called *My Country and the World*.

ANDREI D. SAKHAROV

Progress, Coexistence and Intellectual Freedom

Translated from the Russian
by the *New York Times*

With Introduction, Afterword and Notes
by Harrison E. Salisbury

PENGUIN BOOKS

Penguin Books Ltd, Harmondsworth, Middlesex, England
Penguin Books Inc., 7110 Ambassador Road, Baltimore, Maryland 21207, U.S.A.
Penguin Books Australia Ltd, Ringwood, Victoria, Australia
Penguin Books Canada Ltd, 41 Steelcase Road West, Markham, Ontario, Canada
Penguin Books (N.Z.) Ltd, 182–190 Wairau Road, Auckland 10, New Zealand

—

First published in the U.S.A. 1968
First published in Great Britain by André Deutsch 1968
Published in Pelican Books 1969
Reprinted 1976

—

Copyright © The New York Times Company, 1968

—

Made and printed in Great Britain
by C. Nicholls & Company Ltd
Set in Linotype Times

Contents

Introduction

By Harrison E. Salisbury

ON 6 August 1945, the day the bomb exploded at Hiroshima, Andrei Dimitriyevich Sakharov was twenty-four years old and a student at the Lebedev Institute of Physics in Moscow, one of a handful of remarkable young physicists working with the future Nobel prize-winner Dr Igor Y. Tamm.

Andrei Sakharov was perhaps the most brilliant of a brilliant group. Only a month past his twentieth birthday when Hitler's attack propelled Russia into World War II he, unlike millions of other young Russians, was not called to military duty. The promise of his scholarship was already so great that he was exempted from the army and continued his studies without interruption. In 1942 he graduated from Moscow University with honours in physics and joined the Tamm group at the Lebedev Institute.

Exactly when and how Sakharov learned of Hiroshima is not certain, for the news was suppressed for a time by the Soviet press, and when it was published its significance was minimized. Stalin's censorship was rigid and Hiroshima was not at all to his taste. It came just as – in accordance with promises made at Yalta and reaffirmed at Potsdam – he was about to hurl his Far Eastern armies against Japan. Hiroshima confronted him with a critical dilemma : he had to act with utmost speed or he would not be able to get in against Japan for the kill, and the opportunity for redressing Russia's defeat by Japan in the war of 1905 would be lost.

Although Stalin had ordered the development of an

atom bomb possibly as early as 1942 he probably did not entirely appreciate the implications of Hiroshima. But for young Sakharov and the other physicists of Russia its meaning was dazzlingly clear.

Hiroshima, they knew, had transformed the world. It would never again be the same. The balance of forces had irrevocably shifted. All a scientist at the Lebedev Institute had to know was that an A-bomb had been exploded to perceive that the postulates upon which human society had rested until that moment had become obsolete. No longer did we live in a Communist world, a Capitalist world, a Socialist world, a Feudal world. We lived in a Nuclear world.

The Hiroshima fireball changed the existence of Soviet physicists very specifically. Overnight they were plunged into the frantic task of attempting to match America's possession of the ultimate weapon. The Tamm group was not directly involved in the frenetic endeavour to produce a Soviet A-bomb before the United States – as Stalin deeply feared – used its nuclear weapons to impose upon the world and the Soviet Union an 'American diktat'. This project was placed in the hands of the Soviet Police Chief Lavrenti P. Beria, working in part with scientists and engineers in special prison laboratories, in part with captured German scientists, in part with espionage data, and, of course, with the major burden borne by the fine corps of theoretical physicists which already existed in Russia. The Tamm group was engaged in research which was to have even greater potential in the future. Fission physics was not Tamm's speciality nor was it that of his remarkable young disciple Sakharov. Tamm was Russia's leading scientist in the field of quantum mechanics. Working under Tamm, Sakharov at the incredible age of twenty-six won his doctorate in physics – the Russian doctorate differs from the American Ph.D. The Russian degree is usually awarded to middle-aged men who have spent fifteen or twenty years in gruelling scholarship. The subject of Sakharov's doctorate was cosmic ray research, and in the same year of 1947 his first major scientific contribution appeared in the Soviet Academy of Science's *Journal of Experimental and Theoretical Physics*, on the 'generation of the hard component of cosmic rays'. This paper probably was drawn from his doctoral dissertation.

Within a year he had published two more brilliant contributions to theoretical physics. One was a study of the interaction of an electron and a positron in the production of pairs and the other was a paper which prophetically foreshadowed the shape of the contribution he was about to make – a report on the temperature of excitation in plasma of a gaseous discharge.

This abstruse work marked the movement of Sakharov's talent into the critical field of thermonuclear reactions, of fusion physics, of the H-bomb, and of what lay beyond.

And 1948 marked the last year in which Sakharov's theoretical and innovatory studies would be openly published in Soviet physical journals for many years.

What had happened was this: while the Beria teams pushed ahead towards the production of fission weapons (the A-bomb, an achievement which they attained late in 1949), Sakharov and Tamm (principally Sakharov) leapfrogged ahead towards the hydrogen weapon. Many Soviet scientists contributed to the Russian H-bomb but Sakharov's contribution was the greatest. This must be deduced by circumstance, for Soviet security still conceals the magnitude of Sakharov's discoveries. But at the age of thirty-two he was elected to the Soviet

Academy of Sciences, an honour that has virtually no precedent in Soviet science. His friend, counsellor, collaborator, and teacher, Dr Tamm, was elected a member the same year, but only (and typically) after twenty years as a probationary or corresponding member.

It may not be entirely correct to say, as some Russians do, that Sakharov was the 'father' of the Russian H-bomb; but there is no doubt that he was importantly concerned in it. The measure of his achievement is underlined by the fact that while Russia started far behind the United States in nuclear research she was able to catch up and surpass the Americans in developing the hydrogen bomb. The first Soviet experiments in hydrogen fusion occurred months before those of the United States. Sakharov was responsible for this.

It is important to measure the magnitude of what Sakharov did in order to understand the position which this remarkable man now holds in the Soviet Union. He is, in a sense, a kind of Oppenheimer, Teller, and Hans Bethe all rolled into one. He speaks with a voice at least equal to the sum of all three and, perhaps, even more powerfully, since his achievement was greater and more critical. In 1945 the Soviet Union lay at the mercy of the American A-bomb. Less than a decade later she had matched the United States in nuclear weaponry and produced the first H-bomb ahead of her rival for world power. The debt of the Kremlin to Soviet physics and, specifically, to Sakharov is immeasurable.

The security controls imposed by the nature of Sakharov's research caused his name to disappear from the theoretical journals after 1948, but it is known that 1950 was the breakthrough year. This was the year in which he and Dr Tamm established the theoretical laws of controlled thermonuclear fusion – the means for harnessing the power of the hydrogen atom for the generation of electricity and other peaceful purposes. This work gave him a Stalin prize and was part of the general body of research which won Dr Tamm a share of the Nobel prize for physics in 1958.

Not until 1958 did the name of Andrei Sakharov re-enter the public world. In 1957 he had been permitted to publish a scientific paper in the *Journal of Experimental and Theoretical Physics*, a short work on U-meson reactions in hydrogen, which he wrote with his colleague Yakov B. Zeldovich. This was a sure sign that his security classification had been revised. The next year he made his public debut in the role of social critic of the Soviet order.

By this time Nikita Khrushchev had come to power. He had delivered his famous 'secret speech' against Stalin's crimes in 1956 and the atmosphere within the Soviet Union had begun to ease. For the first time in decades Russians were expressing their views on controversial issues and getting them before the public – although not without difficulty.

The question which Sakharov chose for making his public stand is a revealing one. It concerned the manner in which the state was to educate the specially gifted child. Khrushchev, in what many Russians thought was an anti-intellectual gambit, had launched a programme for revising the Soviet educational system. The Khrushchev proposals called for a strong infusion of 'practical' work into Soviet education. All senior pupils would be required to spend one third of their school time in field or factory work, either interrupting their education entirely or taking on part-time jobs at the age of fifteen or sixteen. The Khrushchev plan retained special schools for gifted children in the arts but left open the question of special training for pupils with unusual talent in mathematics and the sciences.

Sakharov and his close friend and colleague Zeldovich strongly urged that rather than delay the education of gifted youngsters, their training be accelerated through special schools and special courses so that they could enter university work at the age of sixteen or seventeen, one or two years earlier than normal.

The two scientists argued that in mathematics and physics many of the most valuable discoveries were made between the ages of twenty-two and twenty-six and that the younger years were the most productive. The two men did not cite themselves as examples, but it was well known in Soviet scientific and educational circles that the arguments they advanced were strongly supported by the facts of their own careers, particularly that of Sakharov.

Sakharov and Zeldovich not only urged the establishment of special schools for the gifted, but also recommended radical revision in the curriculum of Soviet mathematics in order to bring it into line with the needs of contemporary science and technology. They proposed the abandonment of Euclidean geometry and less emphasis on individual algebraic problems and complex application of trigonometric functions. Instead, they advocated the introduction of subjects related to contemporary applications – the theory of probability, analytic geometry, calculus, and vector analysis.

The question of educational reforms touched off one of the first and most far-reaching open debates of the post-Stalin era. The result was a compromise. For two or three years there was much talk of 'practical work' and hundreds of thousands of youngsters were diverted temporarily to factories and farms, thereby helping to ease an acute labour shortage caused by the sharp war-time drop in the Russian birthrate. At the same time the Sakharov-Zeldovich proposals for gifted scientific students became the criteria for a revitalization of mathematics and science teaching in the Soviet schools. Mathematics had always held a position of highest priority. Now it was regenerated and, as a Moscow school director said recently: 'It's in mathematics that we have all our best arguments.' Mathematics and the theoretical principles opened up by the new mathematics came to be seen by Soviet intellectuals as providing the theoretical foundations for the evolution of a new kind of society.

Despite Sakharov's emergence into public view he was still deeply involved in high-security, military-oriented Soviet research. You will search the indexes of Soviet physical journals and the annals of the Academy of Science in vain in these years for any contribution by him. This is not an indication that the brilliance of his mind had dimmed or that the fertility of his genius had weakened. It simply meant that he was still at work in weapons-related and security-sensitive areas.

But the evolution of his thinking and the formation of his philosophy with respect to basic social questions continued although, naturally, his orientation still tended to lie within a scientific frame of reference.

In the early 1960s Sakharov emerged as a critic of Soviet eclectic genetics and a strong supporter of the classical school based on the theories of Mendel and Morgan. The Mendel-Morgan school holds that genes play the leading role in transmitting the characteristics of plants and animal life.

By entering this controversy Sakharov committed himself to the liberal and progressive side of a politico-scientific conflict which has envenomed nearly twenty-five years of Soviet life and has sent many outstanding Soviet scientists to exile or death.

The fight revolved around the theories of a pragmatic Russian plant breeder named Ivan V. Michurin, a kind of Russian Burbank, who believed that environment could change the heredity of plants. For example, by exposing wheat seeds to cold, he contended, a strain more resistant to cold might be developed.

Michurin died in 1935 but his theories were taken up and elaborated by a ruthless and ambitious agricultural specialist named Trofim D. Lysenko. Lysenko won Stalin's support and utilized his own version of Michurinism to establish a kind of Stalinist dictatorship of the sciences. He succeeded in destroying classical Soviet genetics, poisoned the fields of Soviet agronomy, biology, and botany, and by the time of Stalin's death was on the way towards extending his personal dictatorship over most of the scientific community. With the aid of Stalin and Stalin's police Lysenko sent many brilliant men to prison, to labour camps, and to the execution wall.

Stalin's death gradually brought an end to Lysenko's dictatorship. Pure science began to revive. Lysenko and many of his sycophants were removed from key positions. But so strong was their hold and so persuasive their arguments (basically, that they possessed a short-cut in solving Russia's perennial agricultural problem of poor crops and low yields) that the battle did not cease. In the early 1960s Lysenko made a brief comeback under Khrushchev. In 1963 and 1964 Lysenko again was removed from power but the row went on.

It was at this point that Sakharov joined forces with two specialists on agricultural questions, V. P. Efroim-

son, an expert on silkworm culture, and F. D. Shchepot-
yev, a forester, as well as many classical geneticists, to
attack the persistence of Lysenkoism and Michurinism
in Soviet science and to blame it for the shocking manner in which Soviet genetics and biology lagged behind
the West.

Mikhail A. Olshansky, the president of the Soviet
Agricultural Academy, rebuked Sakharov and his associates for their attacks. But public criticism did not
silence Sakharov. The campaign for freedom of science
from political interference and against the establishment
of a 'state doctrine' of science continued.

The aid of Sakharov and other physicists was instru-
mental in winning for biology and other life sciences the
immunity from political and doctrinaire interference
which had already been won by the physical sciences.

The year 1965 marks a watershed for Sakharov. He
was forty-four years old in 1965. He had been for twelve
years at the pinnacle of Soviet science, a revered member
of the Academy, the holder of unmatched honours for
his role in the creation of the hydrogen bomb.

Whether at this point in the evolution of his thinking
Sakharov, like so many of his physicist colleagues in the
West, decided to cut his ties with military-oriented research and classified projects is not certain. If so, the
precedent had been earlier set by several of the greatest
of Russian physicists, the most important among them
being Peter Kapitsa who rather than work on the A-bomb
under Stalin had submitted to house arrest and the loss
of his laboratory facilities.

In any event, beginning in 1965 Sakharov's name appeared more and more often in the scientific journals –
two articles in 1965, two in 1966, and two in 1967. The
subjects were far beyond the comprehension of popular

readers ('Magnetic cumulation', 'Violation of CP invariance, C asymmetry, and baryon asymmetry of the universe', 'The Quark structure and masses of strongly interacting particles'). There was a shift in the thrust of his interest and theory. In 1965 he published a paper on 'the initial stage of an expanding universe and the appearance of a non-uniform distribution of matter'. His mind had turned to the Quark phenomenon and other questions relating to the universe. His focus was moving away from intensive study of the most minute fragments of matter and energy to a concentration on the totality of the universal structure.

As his scientific preoccupations moved from minute, narrow, intensive concentration on sub-micro elements to the macro-world of the total universe, so his social interest moved from questions intimately concerned with science to broad issues which involved the community as a whole.

The subject which now engaged his attention was one which had been prominent in the minds of Soviet intellectuals since 1956, since Khrushchev's spectacular denunciation of Stalin and the subsequent progressive but erratic and uneven liberalization of Soviet life. By 1966 Khrushchev had been removed from power. His successors were middle-of-the-road bureaucrats. The Communist party was preparing for its Twenty-third Congress and Moscow was buzzing with rumours that the work of de-Stalinization was to be in considerable measure undone, that the hard-liners, the tough-minded, thick-skinned bureaucrats who had risen to power under Stalin and who still constituted the backbone of the Soviet party and government structure, were going to 'rehabilitate' Stalin, at least in part, and under the banner of this cause begin the process of turning the clock back as far as they could towards the Stalin era, reinstating police rule and repression.

It was a measure of how far the Soviet Union had progressed since Stalin's death in 1953 that rumours and reports of these proposals aroused active, vigorous, and widespread opposition. It was a measure of how far the brilliant physicist had progressed towards becoming the brilliant publicly concerned man that Sakharov placed himself at the forefront of the fight against any compromise with neo-Stalinism.

A letter bearing the signatures of twenty-five outstanding names in the world of Soviet intellect and art was sent to Leonid I. Brezhnev, the Party's first secretary. It was signed by Sakharov and four other major Soviet physicists, including Peter Kapitza and Igor Y. Tamm, two brilliant older Soviet liberal writers, Konstantin G. Paustovsky and Viktor Nekrasov, several artistic figures like the prima ballerina Maya Plisetskaya, and the movie director Mikhail I. Romm, and the grand old man of Soviet diplomacy, Ivan M. Maisky, one-time ambassador to London and close friend and colleague of the late Maxim Litvinov.

The twenty-five declared that the Soviet people would never accept any modification of Khrushchev's condemnation of Stalin and that no argument could make them believe the exposure of Stalin's crimes was unjustified. Any step toward rehabilitation of Stalin, they said, would produce a new split between the Communist parties of the West and the Soviet party at a time of growing complications with the United States on the one hand and the Chinese Communist party on the other.

Any step back to Stalin, they warned, 'would be a great disaster.'

Whether the argument of the twenty-five was compelling is not known. What is known is that despite a few flourishes by minor orators no rehabilitation of Stalin, minor or major, was undertaken by the Twenty-third Party Congress.

But the struggle over the future of the Soviet Union and the course which its society should take was only beginning. The role of Academician Sakharov as a critic of that society, of the policies of his government, of the direction in which the world as a whole is moving, was only on the threshold.

From his debut as a teen-age genius, then as a creator of the H-bomb, as a thoughtful critic of educational theory and practice, as an opponent of obscurantism and ideological government interference in science, as an articulate spokesman for dissent in a half-closed society, Sakharov now became a philosopher and social architect on a world scale. He emerged as a man capable not only of searching and precise analysis of forces and counter-forces within the Soviet Union but of the political, social, scientific, and technological stress lines of the world as a whole, a man capable not only of succinct criticism but of originating a concept of social architecture capable of containing and moderating the disruptive and explosive tendencies which have brought humanity, in his considered view, to the brink of extinction.

Like men of science in all countries, Sakharov has peered deeply into the future and cast his glance back to the present. What he sees in the Soviet Union, in America, in China, in the world at large, convinces him that unless the great nations act promptly and together there will be no future.

The American nuclear scientists have long presented the future in terms of a symbolic clock, the hands of which stand at a few minutes to midnight, the hour at which the world destroys itself. Sakharov tells time by the same clock. From the sense of urgency which this clock imparts he derives his concept of a world society in which the peril point may be permanently stayed.

Sakharov's dream of a better world comes to humanity at a moment of deep crisis, at a moment when the clatter of Soviet tanks in the ancient squares of Prague threaten once again to turn Mankind back to the terrible paths of war and conflict.

Sakharov himself may be caught up in the evil currents set in motion by Moscow's act. Even now the prison van may await him. But in this dark hour his voice rises above the tumult proclaiming to East and West:

Act now or perish!

General Statement

THE views of the author were formed in the milieu of the scientific and scientific-technological intelligentsia, which manifests much anxiety over the principles and specific aspects of foreign and domestic policy and over the future of mankind. This anxiety is nourished, in particular, by a realization that the scientific method of directing policy, the economy, arts, education, and military affairs still has not become a reality.

We regard as 'scientific' a method based on deep analysis of facts, theories, and views, presupposing unprejudiced, unfearing open discussion and conclusions. The complexity and diversity of all the phenomena of modern life, the great possibilities and dangers linked with the scientific-technical revolution and with a number of social tendencies demand precisely such an approach, as has been acknowledged in a number of official statements.[1]

In this essay, advanced for discussion, the author has set himself the goal to present, with the greatest conviction and frankness, two theses that are supported by many people in the world. The theses relate to the destruction threatened by the division of mankind and the need for intellectual freedom.

ONE

'The Division of Mankind
Threatens it with Destruction'

1

THE division of mankind threatens it with destruction. Civilization is imperilled by: a universal thermonuclear war, catastrophic hunger for most of mankind, stupefaction from the narcotic of 'mass culture', and bureaucratized dogmatism, a spreading of mass myths that put entire peoples and continents under the power of cruel and treacherous demagogues, and destruction or degeneration from the unforseeable consequences of swift changes in the conditions of life on our planet.

In the face of these perils, any action increasing the division of mankind, any preaching of the incompatibility of world ideologies and nations is madness and a crime. Only universal cooperation under conditions of intellectual freedom and the lofty moral ideals of socialism and labour, accompanied by the elimination of dogmatism and pressures of the concealed interests of ruling classes, will preserve civilization.

The reader will understand that ideological collaboration cannot apply to those fanatical, sectarian, and extremist ideologies that reject all possibility of *rapprochement*, discussion, and compromise, for example, the ideologies of Fascist, racist, militaristic, and Maoist demagogy.[2]

Millions of people throughout the world are striving to put an end to poverty. They despise oppression, dogmatism, and demagogy (and their more extreme manifestations – racism, Fascism, Stalinism, and Maoism). They believe in progress based on the use, under conditions of social justice and intellectual freedom, of all the positive experience accumulated by mankind.

'Intellectual Freedom is Essential'

2

THE second basic thesis is that intellectual freedom is essential to human society – freedom to obtain and distribute information, freedom for open-minded and un-fearing debate and freedom from pressure by officialdom and prejudices. Such a trinity of freedom of thought is the only guarantee against an infection of people by mass myths, which, in the hands of treacherous hypocrites and demagogues, can be transformed into bloody dictatorship. Freedom of thought is the only guarantee of the feasibility of a scientific democratic approach to politics, economy, and culture.[3]

But freedom of thought is under a triple threat in modern society – from the opium of mass culture, from cowardly, egotistic and narrow-minded ideologies, and from the ossified dogmatism of a bureaucratic oligarchy and its favourite weapon, ideological censorship. Therefore, freedom of thought requires the defence of all thinking and honest people. This is a mission not only for the intelligentsia but for all strata of society, particularly its most active and organized stratum, the working class. The worldwide dangers of war, famine, cults of personality, and bureaucracy – these are perils for all of mankind.

Recognition by the working class and the intelligentsia of their common interests has been a striking phenomenon of the present day. The most progressive internationalist, and dedicated element of the intelligentsia is, in essence, part of the working class, and the most advanced, educated, internationalist, and broad-minded part of the working class is part of the intelligentsia.

This position of the intelligentsia in society renders senseless any loud demands that the intelligentsia subordinate its strivings to the will and interests of the working class (in the Soviet Union, Poland, and other socialist countries). What these demands really mean is subordination to the will of the party or, even more specifically, to the party's central apparatus and its officials. Who will guarantee that these officials always express the genuine interests of the working class as a whole and the genuine interests of progress rather than their own caste interests?

We will divide this essay into two parts. The first we will title 'Dangers', and the second, 'The Basis of Hope'.

DANGERS

DANGERS

The Threat of Nuclear War

THREE technical aspects of thermonuclear weapons have made thermonuclear war a peril to the very existence of humanity. These aspects are: the enormous destructive power of a thermonuclear explosion, the relative cheapness of rocket-thermonuclear weapons, and the practical impossibility of an effective defence against a massive rocket-nuclear attack.

1

Today one can consider a three-megaton nuclear warhead as 'typical' (this is somewhere between the warhead of a Minuteman and of a Titan II). The area of fires from the explosion of such a warhead is 150 times greater than from the Hiroshima bomb, and the area of destruction is thirty times greater. The detonation of such a warhead over a city would create a 100-square-kilometre [40 square-mile] area of total destruction and fire.

Tens of millions of square metres of living space would be destroyed. No fewer than a million people would perish under the ruins of buildings, from fire and radiation, suffocate in the dust and smoke or die in shelters buried under debris. In the event of a ground-level explosion, the fallout of radioactive dust would create a danger of fatal exposure in an area of tens of thousands of square kilometres.

2

A few words about the cost and the possible number of explosions.

After the stage of research and development has been passed, mass production of thermonuclear weapons and carrier rockets is no more complex and expensive than, for example, the production of military aircraft, which were produced by the tens of thousands during the war.

The annual production of plutonium in the world now is in the tens of thousands of tons. If one assumes that half this output goes for military purposes and that an average of several kilograms of plutonium goes into one warhead, then enough warheads have already been accumulated to destroy mankind many times over.

3

The third aspect of thermonuclear peril (along with the power and cheapness of warheads) is what we term the practical impossibility of preventing a massive rocket attack. This situation is well known to specialists. In the popular scientific literature, for example, one can read this in an article by Richard L. Garwin and Hans A. Bethe in the *Scientific American* of March 1968.

The technology and tactics of attack have now far surpassed the technology of defence despite the development of highly manoeuvrable and powerful antimissiles with nuclear warheads and despite other technical ideas, such as the use of laser rays and so forth.

Improvements in the resistance of warheads to shock waves and to the radiation effects of neutron and X-ray exposure, the possibility of mass use of relatively light and inexpensive decoys that are virtually indistinguishable from warheads and exhaust the capabilities of an antimissile defence system, a perfection of tactics of massed and concentrated attacks, in time and space, that overstrain the defence detection centres, the use of orbital and fractional-orbital attacks, the use of active and passive jamming, and other methods not disclosed in the press – all this has created technical and economic obstacles to an effective missile defence that, at the present time, are virtually insurmountable.

The experience of past wars shows that the first use of a new technical or tactical method of attack is usually highly effective even if a simple antidote can soon be developed. But in a thermonuclear war the first blow may be the decisive one and render null and void years of work and billions spent on creation of antimissile system.

An exception to this would be the case of a great technical and economic difference in the potentials of two enemies. In such a case, the stronger side, creating an antimissile defence system with a multiple reserve, would face the temptation of ending the dangerous and unstable balance once and for all by embarking on a preemptive adventure, expending part of its attack potential on destruction of most of the enemy's launching bases and counting on impunity for the last stage of escalation, i.e., the destruction of the cities and industry of the enemy.

Fortunately for the stability of the world, the difference between the technical-economic potentials of the Soviet Union and the United States is not so great that one of the sides could undertake a 'preventive aggression' without an almost inevitable risk of a destructive retaliatory blow. This situation would not be changed by a broadening of the arms race through the development of antimissile defences.

In the opinion of many people, an opinion shared by the author, a diplomatic formulation of this mutually comprehended situation, for example, in the form of a moratorium on the construction of antimissile systems, would be a useful demonstration of a desire of the Soviet Union and the United States to preserve the *status quo* and not to widen the arms race for senselessly expensive antimissile systems. It would be a demonstration of a desire to cooperate, not to fight.

A thermonuclear war cannot be considered a continuation of politics by other means (according to the formula of Clausewitz). It would be a means of universal suicide.

Two kinds of attempts are being made to portray thermonuclear war as an 'ordinary' political act in the eyes of public opinion. One is the concept of the 'paper tiger', the concept of the irresponsible Maoist adventurists. The other is the strategic doctrine of escalation, worked out by scientific and militarist circles in the United States. Without minimizing the seriousness of the challenge inherent in that doctrine, we will just note that the political strategy of peaceful coexistence is an effective counter-weight to the doctrine.

A complete destruction of cities, industry, transport, and systems of education, a poisoning of fields, water, and air by radioactivity, a physical destruction of the larger part of mankind, poverty, barbarism, a return to savagery, and a genetic degeneracy of the survivors under the impact of radiation, a destruction of the material and information basis of civilization – this is a measure of the peril that threatens the world as a result of the estrangement of the world's two superpowers.

Every rational creature, finding itself on the brink of a disaster, first tries to get away from the brink and only then does it think about the satisfaction of its other needs. If mankind is to get away from the brink, it must overcome its divisions.

A vital step would be a review of the traditional method of international affairs, which may be termed 'empirical-competitive'. In the simplest definition, this is a method aiming at maximum improvement of one's position everywhere possible and, simultaneously, a method of causing maximum unpleasantness to opposing forces without consideration of common welfare and common interests.[4]

If politics were a game of two gamblers, then this would be the only possible method. But where does such a method lead in the present unprecedented situation?

Vietnam and The Middle East

IN Vietnam, the forces of reaction, lacking hope for an expression of national will in their favour, are using the force of military pressure. They are violating all legal and moral norms and are carrying out flagrant crimes against humanity. An entire people is being sacrificed to the proclaimed goal of stopping the 'Communist tide'.

They strive to conceal from the American people considerations of personal and party prestige, the cynicism and cruelty, the hopelessness and ineffectiveness of the anti-Communist tasks of American policy in Vietnam, as well as the harm this war is doing to the true goals of the American people, which coincide with the universal tasks of bolstering peaceful coexistence.

To end the war in Vietnam would first of all save the people perishing there. But it also is a matter of saving peace in all the world. Nothing undermines the possibilities of peaceful coexistence more than a continuation of the war in Vietnam.[5]

Another tragic example is the Middle East. If direct responsibility on Vietnam rests with the United States, in the Middle East direct responsibility rests not with the United States but with the Soviet Union (and with Britain in 1948 and 1956).

On one hand, there was an irresponsible encouragement of so-called Arab unity (which in no way had a socialist character – look at Jordan – but was purely nationalist and anti-Israel). It was said that the struggle

of the Arabs had an essentially anti-imperialist character. On the other hand, there was an equally irresponsible
encouragement of Israeli extremists.

We cannot here analyse the entire contradictory and
tragic history of the events of the last twenty years,
in the course of which the Arabs and Israel, along with
historically justified actions, carried out reprehensible
deeds, often brought about by the actions of external
forces.

Thus in 1948, Israel waged a defensive war. But in
1956, the actions of Israel appeared reprehensible. The
preventive six-day war in the face of threats of destruction by merciless, numerically vastly superior forces of
the Arab coalition could have been justifiable. But the
cruelty to refugees and prisoners of war and the striving
to settle territorial questions by military means must be
condemned. Despite this condemnation, the breaking of
relations with Israel appears a mistake, complicating a
peaceful settlement in this region and complicating a
necessary diplomatic recognition of Israel by the Arab
governments.[6]

In our opinion, certain changes must be made in the
conduct of international affairs, systematically subor-
dinating all concrete aims and local tasks to the basic
task of actively preventing an aggravation of the international situation, of actively pursuing and expanding
peaceful coexistence to the level of cooperation, of
making policy in such a way that its immediate and
long-range effects will in no way sharpen international
tensions and will not create difficulties for either side
that would strengthen the forces of reaction, militarism,
nationalism, Fascism, and revanchism.

International affairs must be completely permeated
with scientific methodology and a democratic spirit,

with a fearless weighing of all facts, views, and theories, with maximum publicity of ultimate and intermediate goals, and with a consistency of principles.

THREE

International Tensions and New Principles

THE international policies of the world's two leading superpowers (the United States and the Soviet Union) must be based on a universal acceptance of unified and general principles, which we initially would formulate as follows:

1

All peoples have the right to decide their own fate with a free expression of will. This right is guaranteed by international control over observance by all governments of the 'Declaration of the Rights of Man'. International control presupposes the use of economic sanctions as well as the use of military forces of the United Nations in defence of 'the rights of man'.

2

All military and military-economic forms of export of revolution and counter-revolution are illegal and are tantamount to aggression.

3

All countries strive towards mutual help in economic, cultural, and general-organizational problems with the aim of eliminating painlessly all domestic and international difficulties and preventing a sharpening of international tensions and a strengthening of the forces of reaction.

International policy does not aim at exploiting local, specific conditions to widen zones of influence and create difficulties for another country. The goal of international policy is to ensure universal fulfilment of the 'Declaration of the Rights of Man' and to prevent a sharpening of international tension and a strengthening of militarist and nationalist tendencies.

Such a set of principles would in no way be a betrayal of the revolutionary and national liberation struggle, the struggle against reaction and counter-revolution. On the contrary, with the elimination of all doubtful cases, it would be easier to take decisive action in those extreme cases of reaction, racism, and militarism that allow no course other than armed struggle. A strengthening of peaceful coexistence would create an opportunity to avert such tragic events as those in Greece and Indonesia.

Such a set of principles would present the Soviet armed forces with a precisely defined defensive mission, a mission of defending our country and our allies from aggression. As history has shown, our people and their armed forces are unconquerable when they are defending their homeland and its great social and cultural achievements.[7]

FOUR

Hunger and Overpopulation

(and the Psychology of Racism)

SPECIALISTS are paying attention to a growing threat of hunger in the poorer half of the world. Although the fifty per cent increase of the world's population in the last thirty years has been accompanied by a seventy per cent increase in food production, the balance in the poorer half of the world has been unfavourable. The situation in India, Indonesia, in a number of countries of Latin America, and in a large number of other under-developed countries – the absence of technical-economic reserves, competent officials, and cultural skills, social backwardness, a high birthrate – all this systematically worsens the food balance and without doubt will continue to worsen it in the coming years.

The answer would be a wide application of fertilizers, an improvement of irrigation systems, better farm technology, wider use of the resources of the oceans, and a gradual perfection of the production, already technically feasible, of synthetic foods, primarily amino acids. However, this is all fine for the rich nations. In the more backward countries, it is apparent from an analysis of the situation and existing trends that an improvement cannot be achieved in the near future, before the expected date of tragedy, 1975–80.

What is involved is a prognosticated deterioration of the average food balance in which localized food crises merge into a sea of hunger, intolerable suffering and desperation, the grief and fury of millions of people.

This is a tragic threat to all mankind. A catastrophe of such dimension cannot but have profound consequences for the entire world and for every human being. It will provoke a wave of wars and hatred, a decline of standards of living throughout the world, and will leave a tragic, cynical, and anti-Communist mark on the life of future generations.

The first reaction of a Philistine in hearing about the problem is that 'they' are responsible for their plight because 'they' reproduce so rapidly. Unquestionably, control of the birthrate is important and the people, in India for example, are taking steps in this direction. But these steps remain largely ineffective under social and economic backwardness, surviving traditions of large families, an absence of old-age benefits, a high infant mortality rate until quite recently, and a continuing threat of death from starvation.

It is apparently futile only to insist that the more backward countries restrict their birthrates. What is needed most of all is economic and technical assistance to these countries. This assistance must be of such scale and generosity that it is absolutely impossible before the estrangement in the world and the egotistical, narrow-minded approach to relations between nations and races is eliminated. It is impossible as long as the United States and the Soviet Union, the world's two great superpowers, look upon each other as rivals and opponents.

Social factors play an important role in the tragic present situation and the still more tragic future of the poor regions. It must be clearly understood that if a threat of hunger is, along with a striving towards national independence, the main cause of 'agrarian' revolution, the 'agrarian' revolution in itself will not eliminate the threat of hunger, at least not in the immediate future. The threat of hunger cannot be eliminated without the assistance of the developed countries, and this requires significant changes in their foreign and domestic policies.

At this time, the white citizens of the United States are unwilling to accept even minimum sacrifices to eliminate the unequal economic and cultural position of the country's black citizens, who make up ten per cent of the population.

It is necessary to change the psychology of the American citizens so that they will voluntarily and generously support their government and worldwide efforts to change the economy, technology, and level of living of billions of people. This, of course, would entail a serious decline in the United States rate of economic growth. The Americans should be willing to do this solely for the sake of lofty and distant goals, for the sake of preserving civilization and mankind on our planet.

Similar changes in the psychology of people and practical activities of governments must be achieved in the Soviet Union and other developed countries.

In the opinion of the author, a fifteen-year tax equal to twenty per cent of national incomes must be imposed on developed nations. The imposition of such a tax would automatically lead to a significant reduction in expenditures for weapons. Such common assistance would have an important effect – that of stabilizing and improving the situation in the most underdeveloped countries, restricting the influence of extremists of all types.[8]

Changes in the economic situation of underdeveloped countries would solve the problem of high birthrates with relative ease, as has been shown by the experience of developed countries, without the barbaric method of sterilization.

Certain changes in the policies, viewpoints, and traditions on this delicate question are inescapable in the advanced countries as well. Mankind can develop smoothly only if it looks upon itself in a demographic sense as a unit, a single family without divisions into nations other than in matters of history and traditions.

Therefore, government policy, legislation on the family and marriage, and propaganda should not encourage an increase in the birthrates of advanced countries while demanding that it be curtailed in underdeveloped countries that are receiving assistance. Such a two-faced game would produce nothing but bitterness and nationalism.

In conclusion on that point, I want to emphasize that the question of regulating birthrates is highly complex and that any standardized, dogmatic solution 'for all time and all peoples' would be wrong. All the foregoing, incidentally, should be accepted with the reservation that it is somewhat of a simplification.

FIVE

Pollution of Environment

WE live in a swiftly changing world. Industrial and water-engineering projects, cutting of forests, ploughing up of virgin lands, the use of poisonous chemicals – all this is changing the face of the earth, our 'habitat'.

Scientific study of all the interrelationships in nature and the consequences of our interference clearly lag behind the changes. Large amounts of harmful wastes of industry and transport are being dumped into the air and water, including cancer-inducing substances. Will the safe limit be passed everywhere, as has already happened in a number of places?

Carbon dioxide from the burning of coal is altering the heat-reflecting qualities of the atmosphere. Sooner or later, this will reach a dangerous level. But we do not know when. Poisonous chemicals used in agriculture are penetrating the body of man and animal directly and in more dangerous modified compounds, are causing serious damage to the brain, the nervous system, blood-forming organs, the liver, and other organs. Here, too, the safe limit can be easily crossed but the question has not been fully studied and it is difficult to control all these processes.

The use of antibiotics in poultry-raising has led to the development of new disease-causing microbes that are resistant to antibiotics.

I could also mention the problems of dumping detergents and radioactive wastes, erosion and salinization of soils, the flooding of meadows, the cutting of forests on mountain slopes and in watersheds, the destruction of birds and other useful wildlife like toads and frogs, and many other examples of senseless despoliation caused by local, temporary, bureaucratic, and egotistical interest and sometimes simply by questions of bureaucratic prestige, as in the sad fate of Lake Baikal.[9]

The problem of geohygiene (earth hygiene) is highly complex and closely tied to economic and social problems. This problem can therefore not be solved on a national and especially not on a local basis. The salvation of our environment requires that we overcome our divisions and the pressure of temporary, local interests. Otherwise, the Soviet Union will poison the United States with its wastes and vice versa. At present, this is a hyperbole. But with a ten per cent annual increase of wastes, the increase over 100 years will be multiplied 20,000 times.

SIX

Police Dictatorships

AN extreme reflection of the dangers confronting modern social development is the growth of racism, nationalism, and militarism and, in particular, the rise of demagogic, hypocritical, and monstrously cruel dictatorial police regimes. Foremost are the regimes of Stalin, Hitler, and Mao Tse-tung, and a number of extremely reactionary regimes in smaller countries, such as Spain, Portugal, South Africa, Greece, Albania, Haiti, and other Latin American countries.

These tragic developments have always derived from the struggle of egotistical and group interests, the struggle for unlimited power, suppression of intellectual freedom, a spread of intellectually simplified, narrow-minded mass myths (the myth of race, of land and blood, the myth about the Jewish danger, anti-intellectualism, the concept of *lebensraum* in Germany, the myth about the sharpening of the class struggle and proletarian infallibility bolstered by the cult of Stalin and by exaggeration of the contradictions with capitalism in the Soviet Union, the myth about Mao Tse-tung, extreme Chinese nationalism and the resurrection of the *lebensraum* concept, of anti-intellectualism, extreme antihumanism, and certain prejudices of peasant socialism in China).

The usual practice is the use of demagogy, storm troopers, and Red Guards in the first stage and terrorist bureaucracy with reliable *cadres* of the type of Eichmann, Himmler, Yezhov, and Beria at the summit of deification of unlimited power.

The world will never forget the burning of books in the squares of German cities, the hysterical, cannibalistic speeches of the Fascist 'fuehrers', and their even more cannibalistic plans for the destruction of entire peoples, including the Russians. Fascism began a partial realization of these plans during the war it unleashed, annihilating prisoners of war and hostages, burning villages, carrying out a criminal policy of genocide (during the war, the main blow of genocide was aimed at the Jews, a policy that apparently was also meant to be provocative, especially in the Ukraine and Poland).

We shall never forget the kilometre-long trenches filled with bodies, the gas chambers, the S.S. dogs, the fanatical doctors, the piles of women's hair, suitcases with gold teeth, and fertilizer from the factories of death.

Analyzing the causes of Hitler's coming to power, we will never forget the role of German and international monopolist capital. We also will not forget the criminally sectarian and dogmatically narrow policies of Stalin and his associates, setting Socialists and Communists against one another (this has been well related in the famous letter to Ilya Ehrenburg by Ernst Henri).[10]

Fascism lasted twelve years in Germany. Stalinism lasted twice as long in the Soviet Union. There are many common features but also certain differences. Stalinism exhibited a much more subtle kind of hypocrisy and demagogy, with reliance not on an openly cannibalistic programme like Hitler's but on a progressive, scientific, and popular socialist ideology.

This served as a convenient screen for deceiving the working class, for weakening the vigilance of the intellectuals and other rivals in the struggle for power, with the treacherous and sudden use of the machinery of torture, execution, and informants, intimidating and making fools of millions of people, the majority of whom were neither cowards nor fools. As a consequence of this 'specific feature' of Stalinism, it was the Soviet people, its most active, talented, and honest representatives, who suffered the most terrible blow.

At least 10 to 15 million people perished in the torture chambers of the N.K.V.D. [secret police] from torture and execution, in camps for exiled kulaks [rich peasants] and so-called semi-kulaks and members of their families and in camps 'without the right of correspondence' (which were in fact the prototypes of the Fascist death camps where, for example, thousands of prisoners were machine-gunned because of 'overcrowding' or as a result of 'special orders').

People perished in the mines of Norilsk and Vorkuta from freezing, starvation, and exhausting labour, at countless construction projects, in timber-cutting, building of canals, or simply during transportation in prison trains, in the overcrowded holds of 'death ships' in the Sea of Okhotsk, and during the resettlement of entire peoples, the Crimean Tatars, the Volga Germans, the Kalmyks, and other Caucasus peoples. Readers of the literary journal *Novy Mir* recently could read for themselves a description of the 'road of death' between Norilsk and Igarka [in northern Siberia].[11]

Temporary masters were replaced (Yagoda, Molotov, Yezhov, Zhdanov, Malenkov, Beria), but the anti-people's regime of Stalin remained equally cruel and at the same time dogmatically narrow and blind in its cruelty. The killing of military and engineering officials before the war, the blind faith in the 'reasonableness' of the colleague in crime, Hitler, and the other reasons for the national tragedy of 1941 have been well described in the book by Nekrich, in the notes of Maj. Gen.

Grigorenko, and other publications – these are far from the only examples of the combination of crime, narrow-mindedness, and short-sightedness.[12]

Stalinist dogmatism and isolation from real life was demonstrated particularly in the countryside, in the policy of unlimited exploitation and the predatory forced deliveries at 'symbolic' prices, in almost serf-like enslavement of the peasantry, the depriving of peasants of the most simple means of mechanization, and the appointment of collective-farm chairmen on the basis of their cunning and obsequiousness. The results are evident – a profound and hard-to-correct destruction of the economy and way of life in the countryside, which, by the law of interconnected vessels, damaged industry as well.[13]

The inhuman character of Stalinism was demonstrated by the repressions of prisoners of war who survived Fascist camps and then were thrown into Stalinist camps, the anti-worker 'decrees', the criminal exile of entire peoples condemned to slow death, the unenlightened zoological kind of anti-Semitism that was characteristic of Stalinist bureaucracy and the N.K.V.D. (and Stalin personally), the Ukrainophobia characteristic of Stalin, and the draconian laws for the protection of socialist property (five years' imprisonment for stealing some grain from the fields and so forth) that served mainly as a means of fulfilling the demands of the 'slave market').[14]

A profound analysis of the origin and development of Stalinism is contained in the 1,000-page monograph of R. Medvedev. This was written from a socialist, Marxist point of view and is a successful work, but unfortunately it has not yet been published. The present author is not likely to receive such a compliment from

Comrade Medvedev, who finds elements of 'Western-ism' in his views. Well, there is nothing like controversy! Actually the views of the present author are profoundly socialist, and he hopes that the attentive reader will understand this.[15]

The author is quite aware of the monstrous relations in human and international affairs brought forth by the egotistical principle of capital when it is not under pressure from socialist and progressive forces. He also thinks, however, that progressives in the West understand this better than he does and are waging a struggle against these manifestations. The author is concentrating his attention on what is before his eyes and on what is obstructing, from his point of view, a worldwide overcoming of estrangement, obstructing the struggle for democracy, social progress, and intellectual freedom.

Our country has started on the path of cleansing away the foulness of Stalinism. 'We are squeezing the slave out of ourselves drop by drop' (an expression of Anton Chekhov). We are learning to express our opinions, without taking the lead from the bosses and without fearing for our lives.[16]

The beginning of this arduous and far from straight path evidently dates from the report of Nikita S. Khrushchev to the Twentieth Congress of the Soviet Communist party. This bold speech, which came as a surprise to Stalin's accomplices in crime, and a number of associated measures – the release of hundreds of thousands of political prisoners and their rehabilitation, steps towards a revival of the principles of peaceful co-existence and towards a revival of democracy – oblige us to value highly the historic role of Khrushchev despite his regrettable mistakes of a voluntarist character in subsequent years and despite the fact that Khrushchev, while

Stalin was alive, was one of his collaborators in crime, occupying a number of influential posts.[17]

The exposure of Stalinism in our country still has a long way to go. It is imperative, of course, that we publish all authentic documents, including the archives of the N.K.V.D., and conduct nationwide investigations. It would be highly useful for the international authority of the Soviet Communist party and the ideals of socialism if, as was planned in 1964 but never carried out, the party were to announce the 'symbolic' expulsion of Stalin, murderer of millions of party members, and at the same time the political rehabilitation of the victims of Stalinism.

In 1936–9 alone more than 1.2 million party members, half of the total membership, were arrested. Only 50,000 regained freedom; the others were tortured during interrogation or were shot (600,000) or died in camps. Only in isolated cases were the rehabilitated allowed to assume responsible posts; even fewer were permitted to take part in the investigation of crimes of which they had been witnesses or victims.[18]

We are often told lately not to 'rub salt into wounds'. This is usually being said by people who suffered no wounds. Actually only the most meticulous analysis of the past and of its consequences will now enable us to wash off the blood and dirt that befouled our banner.

It is sometimes suggested in the literature that the political manifestations of Stalinism represented a sort of superstructure over the economic basis of an anti-Leninist pseudosocialism that led to the formation in the Soviet Union of a distinct class – a bureaucratic elite from which all key positions are filled and which is rewarded for its work through open and concealed privileges. I cannot deny that there is some (but not the whole) truth in such an interpretation, which would help explain the vitality of neo-Stalinism, but a full analysis of this issue would go beyond the scope of this essay, which focuses on another aspect of the problem.[19]

It is imperative that we restrict in every possible way the influence of neo-Stalinists in our political life. Here we are compelled to mention a specific person. One of the most influential representatives of neo-Stalinism at the present time is the director of the Science Department of the Communist party's Central Committee, Sergei P. Trapeznikov. The leadership of our country and our people should know that the views of this unquestionably intelligent, shrewd, and highly consistent man are basically Stalinist (from our point of view, they reflect the interests of the bureaucratic elite).[20]

His views differ fundamentally from the dreams and aspirations of the majority and most active section of the intelligentsia, which, in our opinion, reflect the true interests of all our people and progressive mankind. The leadership of our country should understand that as long as such a man (if I correctly understand the nature of his views) exercises influence, it is impossible to hope for a strengthening of the party's position among scientific and artistic intellectuals. An indication of this was given at the last elections in the Academy of Sciences when S. P. Trapeznikov was rejected by a substantial majority of votes, but this hint was not 'understood' by the leadership.

The issue does not involve the professional or personal qualities of Trapeznikov, about which I know little. The issue involves his political views. I have based the foregoing on word-of-mouth evidence. Therefore, I cannot in principle exclude the possibility (although it is unlikely) that in reality everything is quite the opposite. In that pleasant event, I would beg forgiveness and retract what I have written.

In recent years, demagogy, violence, cruelty, and vileness have seized a great country that had embarked on the path of socialist development. I refer, of course, to China. It is impossible without horror and pain to read about the mass contagion of antihumanism being spread by 'the great helmsman' and his accomplices, about the Red Guards who, according to the Chinese radio, 'jumped with joy' during public executions of 'ideological enemies' of Chairman Mao.

The idiocy of the cult of personality has assumed in China monstrous, grotesquely tragicomic forms, carrying to the point of absurdity many of the traits of Stalinism and Hitlerism. But this absurdity has proved effective in making fools of tens of millions of people and in destroying and humiliating millions of more honest and more intelligent people.

The full picture of the tragedy in China is unclear. But in any case, it is impossible to look at it in isolation from the internal economic difficulties of China after the collapse of the adventure of 'the great leap forward', in isolation from the struggle by various groups for power, or in isolation from the foreign political situation – the war in Vietnam, the estrangement in the world, and the inadequate and lagging struggle against Stalinism in the Soviet Union.

The greatest damage from Maoism is often seen in the split of the world Communist movement. That is, of course, not so. The split is the result of a disease and to some extent represents the way to treat that disease. In the presence of the disease a formal unity would have been a dangerous, unprincipled compromise that would have led the world Communist movement into a blind alley once and for all.[21]

Actually the crimes of the Maoists against human rights have gone much too far, and the Chinese people are now in much greater need of help from the world's democratic forces to defend their rights than in need of the unity of the world's Communist forces, in the Maoist sense, for the purpose of combatting the so-called imperialist peril somewhere in Africa or in Latin America or in the Middle East.

SEVEN

The Threat to Intellectual Freedom

THIS is a threat to the independence and worth of the human personality, a threat to the meaning of human life.

Nothing threatens freedom of the personality and the meaning of life like war, poverty, terror. But there are also indirect and only slightly more remote dangers.

One of these is the stupefaction of man (the 'grey mass', to use the cynical term of bourgeois prognosticators) by mass culture with its intentional or commercially motivated lowering of the intellectual level and content, with its stress on entertainment or utilitarianism, and with its carefully protective censorship.

Another example is related to the question of education. A system of education under government control, separation of school and church, universal free education – all these are great achievements of social progress. But everything has a reverse side. In this case it is excessive standardization, extending to the teaching process itself, to the curriculum, especially in literature, history, civics, geography, and to the system of examinations.

One cannot but see a danger in excessive reference to authority and in the limitation of discussion and intellectual boldness at an age when personal convictions are beginning to be formed. In the old China, the systems of examinations for official positions led to mental stagnation and to the canonizing of the reactionary aspects of Confucianism. It is highly undesirable to have anything like that in a modern society.

Modern technology and mass psychology constantly suggest new possibilities of managing the norms of behaviour, the strivings and convictions of masses of people. This involves not only management through information based on the theory of advertising and mass psychology, but also more technical methods that are widely discussed in the press abroad. Examples are biochemical control of the birthrate, biochemical control of psychic processes and electronic control of such processes.

It seems to me that we cannot completely ignore these new methods or prohibit the progress of science and technology, but we must be clearly aware of the awesome danger to basic human values and to the meaning of life that may be concealed in the misuse of technical and biochemical methods and the methods of mass psychology.

Man must not be turned into a chicken or a rat as in the well-known experiments in which elation is induced electrically through electrodes inserted into the brain. Related to this is the question of the ever-increasing use of tranquillizers and antidepressants, legal and illegal narcotics, and so forth.

We also must not forget the very real danger mentioned by Norbert Wiener in his book *Cybernetics*, namely the absence in cynbernetic machines of stable human norms of behaviour. The tempting, unprecedented power that mankind, or, even worse, a particular group in a divided mankind, may derive from the wise counsels of its future intellectual aides, the artificial 'thinking' automata, may become, as Wiener warned, a fatal trap; the counsels may turn out to be incredibly insidious and, instead of pursuing human objectives, may pursue completely abstract problems that had been transformed in an unforeseen manner in the artificial brain.

Such a danger will become quite real in a few decades if human values, particularly freedom of thought, will not be strengthened, if alienation will not be eliminated.[20]

Let us now return for the dangers of today, to the need for intellectual freedom, which will enable the public at large and the intelligentsia to control and assess all acts, designs, and decisions of the ruling group.

Marx once wrote that the illusion that the 'bosses know everything best' and 'only the higher circles familiar with the official nature of things can pass judgement' was held by officials who equate the public weal with governmental authority.

Both Marx and Lenin always stressed the viciousness of a bureaucratic system as the opposite of a democratic system. Lenin used to say that every cook should learn how to govern. Now the diversity and complexity of social phenomena and the dangers facing mankind have become immeasurably greater; and it is therefore all the more important that mankind be protected against the danger of dogmatic and voluntaristic errors, which are inevitable when decisions are reached in a closed circle of secret advisers or shadow cabinets.

It is no wonder that the problem of censorship (in the broadest sense of the word) has been one of the central issues in the ideological struggle of the last few years. Here is what a progressive American sociologist, Lewis A. Coser, has to say on this point:

It would be absurd to attribute the alienation of many avant-garde authors solely to the battle with the censors; yet one may well maintain that those battles contributed in no mean measure to such alienation. To these authors, the censor came to be the very symbol of the Philistinism, hypocrisy and meanness of bourgeois society.[23]

Many an author who was initially apolitical was drawn to the political left in the United States because the left was in the forefront of the battle against censorship. The close alliance of avant-garde art with avant-garde political and social radicalism can be accounted for, at least in part, by the fact that they came to be merged in the mind of many as a single battle for freedom against all repression.

(I quote from an article by Igor Kon, published in *Novy Mir* in January 1968.)

We are all familiar with the passionate and closely argued appeal against censorship by the oustanding Soviet writer A. Solzhenitsyn. He, as well as G. Vladimov, G. Svirsky, and other writers who have spoken out on the subject, have clearly shown how incompetent censorship destroys the living soul of Soviet literature; but the same applies, of course, to all other manifestations of social thought, causing stagnation and dullness and preventing fresh and deep ideas.[24]

Such ideas, after all, can arise only in discussion, in the face of objections, only if there is a potential possibility of expressing not only true, but also dubious ideas. This was clear to the philosophers of ancient Greece and hardly anyone nowadays would have any doubts on that score. But after fifty years of complete domination over the minds of an entire nation, our leaders seem to fear even allusions to such a discussion.

At this point we must touch on some disgraceful tendencies that have become evident in the last few years. We will cite only a few isolated examples without trying to create a whole picture. The crippling censorship of Soviet artistic and political literature has again been intensified. Dozens of brilliant writings cannot see the light of day. They include some of the best of Solzhenitsyn's works, executed with great artistic and moral force and containing profound artistic and philosophical generalizations. Is this not a disgrace?

Wide indignation has been aroused by the recent decree adopted by the Supreme Soviet of the Russian Republic, amending the Criminal Code in direct contravention of the civil rights proclaimed by our Constitution. [The decree included literary protests among acts punishable under Article 190, which deals with failure to report crimes.][25]

The Daniel–Sinyavsky trial, which has been condemned by the progressive public in the Soviet Union and abroad (from Louis Aragon to Graham Greene) and has compromised the Communist system, has still not been reviewed. The two writers languish in a camp with a strict regime and are being subjected (especially Daniel) to harsh humiliations and ordeals.[26]

Most political prisoners are now kept in a group of camps in the Mordvinian Republic, where the total number of prisoners, including criminals, is about 50,000. According to available information, the regime has become increasingly severe in these camps, with personnel left over from Stalinist times playing an increasing role. It should be said, in all fairness, that a certain improvement has been noted very recently; it is to be hoped that this turn of events will continue.

The restoration of Leninist principles of public control over places of imprisonment would undoubtedly be a healthy development. Equally important would be a complete amnesty of political prisoners, and not just the recent limited amnesty, which was proclaimed on the fiftieth anniversary of the October Revolution as a result of a temporary victory of rightist tendencies in our leadership. There should also be a review of all political trials that are still raising doubts among the progressive public.[27]

Was it not disgraceful to allow the arrest, twelve-month detention without trial, and then the conviction and sentencing to terms of five to seven years of Ginzburg, Galanskov, and others for activities that actually amounted to a defence of civil liberties and (partly, as an example) of Daniel and Sinyavsky personally. The author of these lines sent an appeal to the party's Central Committee on 11 February 1967, asking that the Ginzburg–Galanskov case be closed. He received no reply and no explanations on the substance of the case. It was only later that he heard there had been an attempt (apparently inspired by Semichastny, the former chairman of the K.G.B.) to slander the present writer and several other persons on the basis of inspired false testimony by one of the accused in the Ginzburg–Galanskov case. Subsequently the testimony of that person – Dobrovolsky – was used at the trial as evidence to show that Ginzburg and Galanskov had ties with a foreign anti-Soviet organization, which one cannot help but doubt.

Was it not disgraceful to permit the conviction and sentencing (to three years in camps) of Khaustov and Bukovsky for participation in a meeting in defence of their comrades? Was it not disgraceful to allow persecution, in the best witch-hunt tradition, of dozens of members of the Soviet intelligentsia who spoke out against the arbitrariness of judicial and psychiatric agencies, to attempt to force honourable people to sign false, hypocritical 'retractions', to dismiss and blacklist people, to deprive young writers, editors, and other members of the intelligentsia of all means of existence?[28]

Here is a typical example of this kind of activity.

Comrade B., a woman editor of books on motion pictures, was summoned to the party's district committee. The first question was, 'Who gave you the letter in defence of Ginzburg to sign?' 'Allow me not to reply to that question,' she answered.

'All right, you can go, we want to talk this over,' she was told.

The decision was to expel the woman from the party and to recommend that she be dismissed from her job and barred from working anywhere else in the field of culture.

With such methods of persuasion and indoctrination the party can hardly expect to claim the role of spiritual leader of mankind.

Was it not disgraceful to have the speech at the Moscow party conference by the president of the Academy of Sciences [Mstislav V. Keldysh], who is evidently either too intimidated or too dogmatic in his views? Is it not disgraceful to allow another backsliding into anti-Semitism in our appointments policy (incidentally, in the highest bureaucratic elite of our government, the spirit of anti-Semitism was never fully dispelled after the nineteen-thirties).[29]

Was it not disgraceful to continue to restrict the civil rights of the Crimean Tatars, who lost about forty-six per cent of their numbers (mainly children and old people) in the Stalinist repressions? Nationality problems will continue to be a reason for unrest and dissatisfaction unless all departures from Leninist principles are acknowledged and analysed and firm steps are taken to correct mistakes.[30]

Is it not highly disgraceful and dangerous to make increasingly frequent attempts, either directly or indirectly (through silence), to publicly rehabilitate Stalin, his associates, and his policy, his pseudosocialism of terroristic bureaucracy, a socialism of hypocrisy and ostentatious growth that was at best a quantitative and one-sided growth involving the loss of many qualitative features? (This is a reference to the basic tendencies and consequences of Stalin's policy, or Stalinism, rather than a comprehensive assessment of the entire diversified situation in a huge country with 200 million people.)

Although all these disgraceful phenomena are still far from the monstrous scale of the crimes of Stalinism and rather resemble in scope the sadly famous McCarthyism of the cold war era, the Soviet public cannot but be highly disturbed and indignant and display vigilance even in the face of insignificant manifestations of neo-Stalinism in our country.[31]

We are convinced that the world's Communists will also view negatively any attempts to revive Stalinism in our country, which would, after all, be an awful blow to the attractive force of Communist ideas throughout the world.

Today the key to a progressive restructuring of the system of government in the interests of mankind lies in intellectual freedom. This has been understood, in particular, by the Czechoslovaks and there can be no doubt that we should support their bold initiative, which is so valuable for the future of socialism and all mankind. That support should be political and, in the early stages, include increased economic aid.[32]

The situation involving censorship (Glavlit) in our country is such that it can hardly be corrected for any length of time simply by 'liberalized' directives. Major organizational and legislative measures are required; for example, adoption of a special law on press and information that would clearly and convincingly define what can and what cannot be printed and would place the responsibility on competent people who would be under public control. It is essential that the exchange of information on an international scale (press, tourism, and so forth) be expanded in every way, that we get to know ourselves better, that we do not try to save on socio-logical, political, and economic research and surveys, which should be conducted not only according to government-controlled programmes (otherwise we might be tempted to avoid 'unpleasant' subjects and questions).

Peaceful Competition

THE prospects of socialism now depend on whether socialism can be made attractive, whether the moral attractiveness of the ideas of socialism and the glorification of labour, compared with the egotistical ideas of private ownership and the glorification of capital, will be the decisive factors that people will bear in mind when comparing socialism and capitalism, or whether people will remember mainly the limitations of intellectual freedom under socialism or, even worse, the fascistic regime of the cult [of personality].

I am placing the accent on the moral aspect because, when it comes to achieving a high productivity of social labour or developing all productive forces or ensuring a high standard of living for most of the population, capitalism and socialism seem to have 'played to a tie'. Let us examine this question in detail.

Imagine two skiers racing through deep snow. At the start of the race, one of them, in striped jacket, was many kilometres ahead, but now the skier in the red jacket is catching up to the leader. What can we say about their relative strength? Not very much, since each skier is racing under different conditions. The striped one broke the snow, and the red one did not have to. (The reader will understand that this ski race symbolizes the burden of research and development costs that the country leading in technology has to bear.) All one can say about the race is that there is not much difference in strength between the two skiers.

The parable does not, of course, reflect the whole complexity of comparing economic and technological progress in the United States and the Soviet Union, the relative vitality of RRS and AME (Russian Revolutionary Sweep and American Efficiency).

We cannot forget that during much of the period in question the Soviet Union waged a hard war and then healed its wounds; we cannot forget that some absurdities in our development were not an inherent aspect of the socialist course of development, but a tragic accident, a serious, though not inevitable, disease.

On the other hand, any comparison must take account of the fact that we are now catching up with the United States only in some of the old, traditional industries, which are no longer as important as they used to be for the United States (for example, coal and steel). In some of the newer fields, for example, automation, computers, petro-chemicals, and especially in industrial research and development, we are not only lagging behind but are also growing more slowly, so that a complete victory of our economy in the next few decades is unlikely.

It must also be borne in mind that our nation is endowed with vast natural resources, from fertile black earth to coal and forest, from oil to manganese and diamonds. It must be borne in mind that during the period under review our people worked to the limit of their capacity, which resulted in a certain depletion of resources.

We must also bear in mind the ski-track effect, in which the Soviet Union adopted principles of industrial organization and technology and development previously tested in the United States. Examples are the method of calculating the national fuel budget,

THE BASIS FOR HOPE

assembly-line techniques, antibiotics, nuclear power, oxygen converters in steel-making, hybrid corn, self-propelled harvester combines, strip-mining of coal, rotary excavators, semiconductors in electronics, the shift from steam to diesel locomotives, and much more.

There is only one justifiable conclusion and it can be formulated cautiously as follows:

1. We have demonstrated the vitality of the socialist course, which has done a great deal for the people materially, culturally, and socially and, like no other system, has glorified the moral significance of labour.

2. There are no grounds for asserting, as is often done in the dogmatic vein, that the capitalist mode of production leads the economy into a blind alley or that it is obviously inferior to the socialist mode in labour productivity, and there are certainly no grounds for asserting that capitalism always leads to absolute impoverishment of the working class.[33]

The continuing economic progress being achieved under capitalism should be a fact of great theoretical significance for any nondogmatic Marxist. It is precisely this fact that lies at the basis of peaceful coexistence and it suggests, in principle, that if capitalism ever runs into an economic blind alley it will not necessarily have to leap into a desperate military adventure. Both capitalism and socialism are capable of long-term development, borrowing positive elements from each other, and actually coming closer to each other in a number of essential aspects.

I can just hear the outcries about revisionism and blunting of the class approach to this issue; I can just see the smirks about political naïvety and immaturity. But the facts suggest that there is real economic progress in the United States and other capitalist countries, that the capitalists are actually using the social principles of socialism, and that there has been real improvement in the position of the working people. More important, the facts suggest that on any other course except ever-increasing coexistence and collaboration between the two systems and the two superpowers, with a smoothing of contradictions and with mutual assistance, on any other course annihilation awaits mankind. There is no other way out.

We will now compare the distribution of personal income and consumption for various social groups in the United States and the Soviet Union. Our propaganda materials usually assert that there is crying inequality in the United States, while the Soviet Union has something entirely just, entirely in the interests of the working people. Actually both statements contain half-truths and a fair amount of hypocritical evasion.

I have no intention of minimizing the tragic aspects of the poverty, lack of rights, and humiliation of the 22 million American Negroes. But we must clearly understand that this problem is not primarily a class problem, but a racial problem, involving the racism and egotism of white workers, and that the ruling group in the United States is interested in solving this problem. To be sure the government has not been as active as it should be; this may be related to fears of an electoral character and to fears of upsetting the unstable equilibrium in the country and thus activating extreme leftist and especially extreme rightist parties. It seems to me that we in the socialist camp should be interested in letting the ruling group in the United States settle the Negro problem without aggravating the situation in the country.

At the other extreme, the presence of millionaires in the United States is not a serious economic burden in view of their small number. The total consumption of the rich is less than twenty per cent, that is, less than the total rise of national consumption over a five-year period. From this point of view, a revolution, which would be likely to halt economic progress for more than five years, does not appear to be an economically advantageous move for the working people. And I am not even talking of the blood-letting that is inevitable in a revolution. And I am not talking of the danger of the 'irony of history', about which Friedrich Engels wrote so well in his famous letter to V. Zasulich, the 'irony' that took the form of Stalinism in our country.

There are, of course, situations where revolution is the only way out. This applies especially to national uprisings. But that is not the case in the United States and other developed capitalist countries, as suggested, incidentally, in the programmes of the Communist parties of these countries.[34]

As far as our country is concerned, here, too, we should avoid painting an idyllic picture. There is still great inequality in property between the city and the countryside, especially in rural areas that lack a transport outlet to the private market or do not produce any goods in demand in private trade. There are great differences between cities with some of the new, privileged industries and those with older, antiquated industries. As a result forty per cent of the Soviet population is in difficult economic circumstances. In the United States about twenty-five per cent of the population is on the verge of poverty. On the other hand the five per cent of the Soviet population that belong to the managerial group is as privileged as its counterpart in the United States.

The development of modern society in both the Soviet

Union and the United States is now following the same course of increasing complexity of structure and of industrial management, giving rise in both countries to managerial groups that are similar in social character.

We must therefore acknowledge that there is no qualitative difference in the structure of society of the two countries in terms of distribution of consumption. Unfortunately the effectiveness of the managerial group in the Soviet Union (and, to a lesser extent, in the United States) is measured not only in purely economic or productive terms. This group also performs a concealed protective function that is rewarded in the sphere of consumption by concealed privileges.

Few people are aware of the practice under Stalin of paying salaries in sealed envelopes, of the constantly recurring concealed distribution of scarce foods and goods for various services, privileges in vacation resorts, and so forth.

I want to emphasize that I am not opposed to the socialist principle of payment based on the amount and quality of labour. Relatively higher wages for better administrators, for highly skilled workers, teachers, and physicians, for workers in dangerous or harmful occupations, for workers in science, culture, and the arts, all of whom account for a relatively small part of the total wage bill, do not threaten society if they are not accompanied by concealed privileges; moreover, higher wages benefit society if they are deserved.[35]

The point is that every wasted minute of a leading administrator represents a major material loss for the economy, and every wasted minute of a leading figure in the arts means a loss in the emotional, philosophical, and artistic wealth of society. But when something is done in secret, the suspicion inevitably arises that things are not clean, that loyal servants of the existing system are being bribed.

It seems to me that the rational way of solving this touchy problem would be not the setting of income ceilings for party members or some such measure, but simply the prohibition of all privileges and the establishment of unified wage rates based on the social value of labour and an economic market approach to the wage problem.

I consider that further advances in our economic reform and a greater role for economic and market factors accompanied by increased public control over the managerial group (which, incidentally, is also essential in capitalist countries) will help eliminate all the roughness in our present distribution pattern.

An even more important aspect of the economic reform for the regulation and stimulation of production is the establishment of a correct system of market prices, proper allocation and rapid utilization of investment funds, and proper use of natural and human resources based on appropriate rents in the interest of our society.

A number of socialist countries, including the Soviet Union, Yugoslavia, and Czechoslovakia are now experimenting with basic economic problems of the role of planning and of the market, government and cooperative ownership, and so forth. These experiments are of great significance.[36]

Summing up, we now come to our basic conclusion about the moral and ethical character of the advantages of the socialist course of development of human society. In our view, this does not in any way minimize the significance of socialism. Without socialism, bourgeois practicism and the egotistical principle of private ownership gave rise to the 'people of the abyss' described by Jack London and earlier by Engels.

Only the competition with socialism and the pressure of the working class made possible the social progress of the twentieth century and, all the more, will ensure the now inevitable process of *rapprochement* of the two systems. It took socialism to raise the meaning of labour to the heights of a moral feat. Before the advent of socialism, national egotism gave rise to colonial oppression, nationalism, and racism. By now it has become clear that victory is on the side of the humanistic, international approach.

The capitalist world could not help giving birth to the socialist, but now the socialist world should not seek to destroy by force the ground from which it grew. Under the present conditions this would be tantamount to suicide of mankind. Socialism should ennoble that ground by its example and other indirect forms of pressure and then merge with it.

The *rapprochement* with the capitalist world should not be an unprincipled, antipopular plot between ruling groups, as happened in the extreme case [of the Soviet-Nazi *rapprochement*] of 1939–40. Such a *rapprochement* must rest not only on a socialist, but on a popular, democratic foundation, under the control of public opinion, as expressed through publicity, elections, and so forth.

Such a *rapprochement* implies not only wide social reforms in the capitalist countries, but also substantial changes in the structure of ownership, with a greater role played by government and cooperative ownership, and the preservation of the basic present features of ownership of the means of production in the socialist countries.

Our allies along this road are not only the working

class and the progressive intelligentsia, which are interested in peaceful coexistence and social progress and in a democratic, peaceful transition to socialism (as reflected in the programmes of the Communist parties of the developed countries), but also the reformist part of the bourgeoisie, which supports such a programme of 'convergence'. (Although I am using this term, taken from the Western literature, it is clear from the foregoing that I have given it a socialist and democratic meaning.)

Typical representatives of the reformist bourgeoisie are Cyrus Eaton, President Franklin D. Roosevelt and, especially, President John F. Kennedy. Without wishing to cast a stone in the direction of Comrade N. S. Khrushchev (our high esteem of his services was expressed earlier), I cannot help recalling one of his statements, which may have been more typical of his entourage than of him personally.

On 10 July 1961, in speaking at a reception of specialists about his meeting with Kennedy in Vienna, Comrade Khrushchev recalled Kennedy's request that the Soviet Union, in conducting policy and making demands, consider the actual possibilities and the difficulties of the new Kennedy Administration and refrain from demanding more than it could grant without courting the danger of being defeated in elections and being replaced by rightist forces. At that time, Khrushchev did not give Kennedy's unprecedented request the proper attention, to put it mildly, and began to rail. And now, after the shots in Dallas, who can say what auspicious opportunities in world history have been, if not destroyed, but, at any rate, set back because of a lack of understanding.[37]

Bertrand Russell once told a peace congress in

Moscow that 'the world will be saved from thermonuclear annihilation if the leaders of each of the two
systems prefer complete victory of the other system to a
thermonuclear war.' (I am quoting from memory.) It
seems to me that such a solution would be acceptable to
the majority of people in any country, whether capitalist
or socialist. I consider that the leaders of the capitalist
and socialist systems by the very nature of things will
gradually be forced to adopt the point of view of the
majority of mankind.

Intellectual freedom of society will facilitate and
smooth the way for this trend towards patience, flexibi-
lity, and a security from dogmatism, fear, and adventurism. All mankind, including its best organized and
active forces, the working class and the intelligentsia, is
interested in freedom and security.

TWO

A Four-stage Plan for Cooperation

HAVING examined in the first part of this essay the development of mankind according to the worse alternative, leading to annihilation, we must now attempt, even schematically, to suggest the better alternative. (The author concedes the primitiveness of his attempts at prognostication, which requires the joint efforts of many specialists, and here, even more than elsewhere, invites positive criticism.)

1

In the first stage, a growing ideological struggle in the socialist countries between Stalinist and Maoist forces, on the one hand, and the realistic forces of leftist Leninist Communists (and leftist Westerners), on the other, will lead to a deep ideological split on an international, national, and intraparty scale.

In the Soviet Union and other socialist countries, this process will lead first to a multiparty system (here and there) and to acute ideological struggle and discussions, and then to the ideological victory of the realists, affirming the policy of increasing peaceful coexistence, strengthening democracy, and expanding economic reforms (1960–80). The dates reflect the most optimistic unrolling of events.

The author, incidentally, is not one of those who consider the multiparty system to be an essential stage in the development of the socialist system or, even less, a panacea for all ills, but he assumes that in some cases a multiparty system may be an inevitable consequence of the course of events when a ruling Communist party refuses for one reason or another to rule by the scientific democratic method required by history.

2

In the second stage, persistent demands for social progress and peaceful coexistence in the United States and other capitalist countries, and pressure exerted by the example of the socialist countries and by internal progressive forces (the working class and the intelligentsia) will lead to the victory of the leftist reformist wing of the bourgeoisie, which will begin to implement a programme of *rapprochement* (convergence) with socialism, i.e., social progress, peaceful coexistence, and collaboration with socialism on a world scale and changes in the structure of ownership. This phase includes an expanded role for the intelligentsia and an attack on the forces of racism and militarism (1972–85). (The various stages overlap.)

3

In the third stage, the Soviet Union and the United States, having overcome their alienation, solve the problem of saving the poorer half of the world. The aforementioned twenty per cent tax on the national income of developed countries is applied. Gigantic fertilizer factories and irrigation systems using atomic power will be built [in the developing countries], the resources of the sea will be used to a vastly greater extent, indigenous personnel will be trained, and industrialization will be carried out. Gigantic factories will produce synthetic

amino acids and synthesize proteins, fats, and carbohydrates. At the same time disarmament will proceed
(1972–90).

4

In the fourth stage, the socialist convergence will reduce
differences in social structure, promote intellectual freedom, science, and economic progress and lead to the creation of a world government and the smoothing of national contradictions (1980 2000). During this period
decisive progress can be expected in the field of nuclear
power, both on the basis of uranium and thorium and,
probably, deuterium and lithium.

Some authors consider it likely that explosive breed-
ing (the reproduction of active materials such as plutonium, uranium 233 and tritium) may be used in sub-
terranean or other enclosed explosions.

During this period the expansion of space exploration
will require thousands of people to work and live con-
tinuously on other planets and on the moon, on artificial
satellites and on asteroids whose orbits will have been
changed by nuclear explosions.

The synthesis of materials that are superconductors
at room temperature may completely revolutionize elec-
trical technology, cybernetics, transportation, and com-
munications. Progress in biology (in this and subsequent
periods) will make possible effective control and direction of all life processes at the levels of the cell, organ-
ism, ecology, and society, from fertility and ageing to
psychic processes and heredity.

If such an all-encompassing scientific and technological revolution, promising uncounted benefits for mankind, is to be possible and safe, it will require the greatest
possible scientific foresight and care and concern for

human values of a moral, ethical, and personal character. (I touched briefly on the danger of a thoughtless
bureaucratic use of the scientific and technological revolution in a divided world in the section on 'Dangers',
but could add a great deal more.) Such a revolution will
be possible and safe only under highly intelligent worldwide guidance.

The foregoing programme presumes:

(a) worldwide interest in overcoming the present divisions;

(b) the expectation that modifications in both the
socialist and capitalist countries will tend to reduce contradictions and differences;

(c) worldwide interest of the intelligentsia, the working class, and other progressive forces in a scientific
democratic approach to politics, economics, and culture;

(d) the absence of insurmountable obstacles to economic development in both world economic systems
that might otherwise lead inevitably into a blind alley,
despair, and adventurism.

Every honourable and thinking person who has not
been poisoned by narrow-minded indifference will seek
to ensure that future development will be along the lines
of the better alternative. However only broad, open discussion, without the pressure of fear and prejudice, will
help the majority to adopt the correct and best course
of action.

THREE

A Summary of Proposals

IN conclusion, I will sum up some of the concrete proposals of varying degrees of importance that have been discussed in the text. These proposals, addressed to the leadership of the country, do not exhaust the content of the article.

1

The strategy of peaceful coexistence and collaboration must be deepened in every way. Scientific methods and principles of international policy will have to be worked out, based on scientific prediction of the immediate and more distant consequences.

2

The initiative must be seized in working out a broad programme of struggle against hunger.

3

A law on press and information must be drafted, widely discussed, and adopted, with the aim not only of ending irresponsible and irrational censorship, but of encouraging self-study in our society, fearless discussion, and the search for truth. The law must provide for the material resources of freedom of thought.

4

All anticonstitutional laws and decrees violating human rights must be abrogated.

5

Political prisoners must be amnestied and some of the recent political trials must be reviewed (for example, the Daniel–Sinyavsky and Ginzburg–Galanskov cases). The camp regime of political prisoners must be promptly relaxed.

6

The exposure of Stalin must be carried through to the end, to the complete truth, and not just to the carefully weighed half-truth dictated by caste considerations. The influence of neo-Stalinists in our political life must be restricted in every way (the text mentioned, as an example, the case of S. Trapeznikov, who enjoys too much influence).

7

The economic reform must be deepened in every way and the area of experimentation expanded, with conclusions based on the results.

8

A law on geohygiene must be adopted after broad discussion, and ultimately become part of world efforts in this area.

With this article the author addresses the leadership of our country and all its citizens as well as all people of goodwill throughout the world. The author is aware of the controversial character of many of his statements. His purpose is open, frank discussion under conditions of publicity.

In conclusion a comment on the text. In the process of discussion of previous drafts of this article, some incomplete and in some respects one-sided texts have been circulated. Some of them contained certain passages that were inept in form and tact and were included through oversight. The author asks readers to bear this in mind. The author is deeply grateful to readers of preliminary drafts who communicated their friendly comments and thus helped improve the essay and refine a number of basic statements.

A. Sakharov

June 1968

Notes

By Harrison E. Salisbury

1. The intelligentsia has traditionally occupied a critical and very special position in Russia, a position and tradition which was crystallized in the nineteenth century, long before the coming to power of the Bolsheviks under Vladimir Lenin in 1917.

The Russian *intelligent,* or member of the intelligentsia, has played a particular role in the evolution of modern Russian society. In the nineteenth century Russia was made up of an enormous mass of peasants, ill-trained and almost universally illiterate; a comparatively small aristocracy, extremely wealthy and often culturally alienated from their own homeland; a small but growing class of entrepreneur industrialists, often drawn from the ranks of avaricious or aggressive peasants; and a thin layer of intelligentsia – university graduates, teachers, doctors, lawyers, writers, poets, scientists, and literate individuals with greater than ordinary education. Possibly because of the widespread illiteracy, possibly because of an ill-defined tradition of service, the Russian intelligentsia took upon itself a social responsibility. It became the germinal force of change and innovation. Generation after generation of Russian writers emerged as the critics of the prevailing despotism of the Tsarist system; generation after generation of Russian students shouldered the responsibility of working for the improvement of the condition of the peasant and the reform of the outmoded Russian state system.

The feeling of social responsibility, of a duty to the state and people, was accentuated by the 1917 Revolution in which the intelligentsia played a leading role. The Bolshevik regime, to some extent under Lenin but increasingly under Stalin, sought to suppress the liberal and critical functions of the intelligentsia and harness its talents to dictated state goals. Writers for example, were assigned by Stalin the function of 'engineers of human souls'; they were ordered to write on topics designated by the state; their works were to be directed towards the achievement of state purposes. The intelligentsia, naturally the freest thinking, most idiosyncratic members of Russian society, suffered more severely than any other class at the hands of Stalin's police.

With the emergence of the more liberal post-Stalin regime the intelligentsia has resumed its old and traditional role as the mainspring of reform and liberal ideals within Russian society. As a class it has grown enormously by the universalization of education and by the stress laid by the Soviet regime upon science, technology, and the arts.

The 'milieu of the scientific and scientific-technological intelligentsia' to which Sakharov refers is in many respects one of the most influential within Soviet society. It comprises the scientists who are responsible for making Russia a nuclear power; who placed the first man into orbit; who gave Russia its intercontinental ballistic missiles; who created the enormous Soviet educational-scientific establishment; who have placed her industry in the forefront of the world, second only to that of the United States. This scientific-technological intelligentsia is closely linked to the artistic intelligentsia – the young poets like Voznesensky and Yevtushenko, the older writers like Pasternak and Ehrenburg, the new classics like Solzhenitsyn.

The appearance publicly or semi-publicly of thoughtful critical analyses of Soviet society emanating from discussions within this milieu has become more and more frequent. The Soviet 'scientific-technological intelligentsia' has been closely linked to the milieu of their counterparts abroad. Most leading Soviet scientists and technologists have attended dozens of conferences and congresses with their foreign colleagues. They visit foreign countries with great frequency, often making one, two, or three trips a year. They are familiar with the main currents of Western (and Eastern) thought, and they are familiar with the reality of social and political conditions in other countries. They can compare not only the reality of Soviet life with the reality of life abroad; they are able to compare the reality of Western life with the caricature of Western life presented in Party propaganda. As so many of these men and women are trained in the scientific process, they are keen and accurate observers. The Sakharov declaration is the product of such observation and thought.

How widely he has circulated his views within his own country is not entirely clear. But numerous references within the document make plain that it was drafted specifically for circulation and for discussion. It would be reasonable to suppose that Sakharov's 'thoughts' are now known to most members of the Academy of Sciences, to most participants in the leading institutes of physics, mathematics, and physical sciences, to a broad cross-section of the University intelligentsia not only in cities like Moscow, Kiev, and Leningrad but in other areas of scientific research, such as the Siberian centres of Novosibirsk and Irkutsk.

The close linkage of the 'scientific-technological intelligentsia' and the artistic intelligentsia would carry the document into this milieu as well. Thus, even before the publication of Sakharov's views in the West, it is probable that they were known in very wide circles of the Soviet Union. With their publication in the West their dissemination in Russia has been vastly increased since most literate Russians now listen to or have access to foreign radio stations. Despite a resumption of jamming of Russian language broadcasts those in English, French, and German continue to be received.

The internal evidence of the document also indicates that this is not the first draft, but that Sakharov has circulated earlier versions and revised them in line with criticisms and suggestions. Indeed, it is implicit in his text that he envisaged further revisions on the basis of broader readership and criticism.

2. Sakharov makes clear from the outset to any reader with Marxist training that his criticism comes from 'within', that is, from within a general Marxist orientation of society, rather than from outside. He establishes this in his first paragraph by stating that his anxiety is stimulated by the realization that the 'scientific' method of directing policy 'still has not become a reality'. This is an allusion to Marx's thesis that his theory provides a 'scientific' method for the analysis and direction of human affairs. In other words, Sakharov is critical not of Marxism, *per se,* but of the failure of Marxists to evolve a scientific method of directing society. His 'thoughts' contain no criticism of the classic hypothesis of Marxism as such; merely devastating criticisms of what so-called Marxists such as Stalin, Mao, and their like have wrought.

To the Soviet reader one of the most dramatic formulations of Sakharov is his equation of Fascism, racism, Stalinism, and Maoism. No official Soviet spokesman has gone so far in condemnation of Stalin as to equate him with the Fascists of Europe or the racists of Alabama and South Africa.

The Soviet reader instantly notes that one of Sakharov's principal thrusts is against the Chinese. In the present context of Soviet-Chinese relations this provides Sakharov with an important doctrinal defence. In other words, Sakharov, in part, justifies his criticism of Soviet policy and his proposals for its reformation upon fear of China's Maoists and the need of meeting the world crisis of communism. The same point was raised in the letter of the twenty-five on the eve of the Twenty-third Party Congress.

3. The demand for intellectual freedom – freedom of information, freedom to speak, freedom to criticize, and freedom from censorship or other official pressures – is central to the demands of the Soviet intelligentsia as expressed with increasing frequency in the last few years. It lies at the heart of the critical letters of Aleksandr Solzhen-

itsyn to the Soviet Writers' Union, protesting against Soviet censorship and Government-Police interference with a writer's tasks; it lay at the root of the conflict between the artists and poets and Nikita Khrushchev in 1962 and 1963; it has been reiterated by Andrei Voznesensky, Yevgeny Yevtushenko, Ilya Ehrenburg, Kornei Chukovsky, and a pleiad of Russian writers.

4. Sakharov's analysis of the devastating results of nuclear warfare, the costs of and simplicity of manufacture of nuclear weapons, and the size of the world nuclear stockpile, coincide precisely with the published documentation of American nuclear scientists. Indeed, his description may well be drawn from publications of the *Bulletin of Atomic Scientists* and similar United States materials since comparable data have not been published publicly in the Soviet Union. His familiarity with American literature in this field is emphasized by his use of the critical article in the March, 1968, *Scientific American*, by the American physicists Richard L. Garwin and Hans A. Bethe, on antimissile systems.

Garwin and Bethe, analysing the capabilities of the Soviet Union and the United States, concluded that the concept of an antimissile system was illusory, that the offence could always remain superior to the defence, and that to go into a new round of missilery would, in the end, cost each nation scores of billions of dollars and leave each still subject to mutual catastrophic destruction.

Summarizing the Garwin-Bethe arguments, Sakharov arrives at the same view as the Americans and concludes that a thermonuclear war cannot be, in the famous definition of the Prussian general and military theorist Karl von Clausewitz, a 'continuation of politics by other means' but, instead, would prove to be a 'means of universal suicide'.

Sakharov's philosophy on this and many other nuclear questions reveals an identity of viewpoint with that of leading American, British, French, and Japanese nuclear physicists. Many of these views have been advanced and discussed in the annual Pugwash conferences, so named for the first meetings sponsored at Pugwash, Nova Scotia, by Cyrus Eaton, the Cleveland industrialist. Sakharov has not personally participated in these meetings but many of his close associates, including Tamm, have done so.

5. Sakharov's characterization of the American war in Vietnam is the classic description of that conflict, as drawn by the Soviet government. There is no difference between his analysis and that advanced by Premier Kosygin and Party Secretary Brezhnev. This is an important point of convergence in official Soviet doctrine and the views of this brilliant critic. It is important not only because it demonstrates an area of agreement between the government policy makers and Sakharov but serves to highlight areas in which the physicist finds himself in basic disagreement. From the standpoint of his relations with the Soviet power structure this fact has special importance. Sakharov can point to Vietnam to demonstrate that his criticism is principled; that it is independent, in the sense that it does not merely repeat the Western viewpoint – liberal or otherwise, and that in major aspects he completely supports basic Soviet positions. Other points which he can cite in this connexion are his posture of criticism *within* rather than *outside* Marxist theory and his concept of Mao and Mao's China as being outside the Communist framework and constituting a kind of Chinese fascism.

6. One of the most interesting and idiosyncratic points of Sakharov's 'thoughts' lies in his analysis of the Israeli question. He supports the Israel war of Independence waged in 1948. It should be recalled that the Soviet Union was the first power in 1948 to recognize the independence of Israel and to establish diplomatic relations, even before the United States – a position of friendship which quickly cooled due to Stalin's anti-Semitism and fears that Israel

had a lien on the loyalty of the 3,500,000 surviving Soviet Jews.

Sakharov condemns unequivocally Israel's participation with England and France in the abortive 1956 attack on Egypt. But he condones Israel's 1967 six-day preventive war against the Arab states and puts full blame upon the Soviet Union for 'irresponsible encouragement' of the Arab states, going out of his way to underline the fact that the efforts of Soviet apologists to give the conflict some kind of a 'socialist character' had no justification.

But, he contends, the Israeli cause lost its just basis by cruel treatment of refugee populations and by seeking a military resolution of territorial questions. He is careful to note that Israeli extremists were encouraged just as irresponsibly as the Arabs.

Nonetheless, the balance of his criticism clearly lies against his own government, against Soviet policy *vis-à-vis* the Arabs, and he is sharp in condemning Moscow for severing relations with Israel, thus further complicating the resolution of the Arab-Israeli conflict.

Writing before the Czech invasion, he seeks to balance the conduct of the United States in Vietnam with the conduct of the Soviet Union in the Middle East.

In criticism of Soviet Middle Eastern policy Sakharov reflects the views of a major segment of Soviet public opinion. It was notable during June and July 1967, that the Soviet public did not share the pro-Arab sentiments prominently proclaimed by *Pravda* and *Izvestiya*. Ordinary citizens in Moscow were enormously impressed with the Israeli military victory and almost universally condemnatory of the Arabs, for whom they had little or no emotional enthusiasm. Many Russians sought at least a participatory measure of glory from the Israeli triumph by coopting the Israeli commander, General Moshe Dayan. The belief was widespread among the Russians that Dayan was, in fact, a Russian Jew who had emigrated to Israel. One rumour made him a graduate of the Voroshilov Military

Academy. Other Russians said of the Israeli success: 'Naturally, the Israelis won; they had three winners of the Order of the Red Banner on their side; the Arabs had only two.'

7. The Declaration of the Rights of Man to which Sakharov refers presumably is that of the French Revolution, although he may have in mind, as well, the 'Universal Declaration of Human Rights' approved in 1948 by the General Assembly of the United Nations. The Rights specified in the 1948 Declaration were embodied in two covenants, the International Covenant on Civil and Political Rights and the International Covenant on Economic, Social, and Cultural Rights adopted by the United Nations General Assembly, 16 December 1966.

The United Nations document, in essence, is a reaffirmation and restatement in more contemporary terms of the principles of the original declaration which, in turn, is closely patterned after the American Declaration of Independence and the Bill of Rights of the American Constitution. It has not, unfortunately, ever been ratified by the United States Senate nor submitted to that body by the State Department.

The United Nations Declaration holds that 'all human beings are born free and equal in dignity and rights' and that everyone is entitled to the rights and freedoms of the Declaration 'without distinction of any kind, such as race, colour, sex, language, religion, political or other opinion, national or social origin, property, birth or other status'.

Sakharov's proposal is to utilize the United Nations as an instrument for the universalization of these basic human rights.

He makes two key points: he proposes that the United Nations employ its military forces in this connexion, and he suggests that by defining the goal as the universalization of human rights the assigned mission of the Soviet armed forces would be defined more precisely.

Several possibilities emerge from these propositions. First, Sakharov's suggestions would provide a justification for the intervention of United Nations forces to enforce civil liberties, say, in Czechoslovakia, in South Africa, or in a new Nazi Germany. They would also justify the intervention of a United Nations force to establish the civil rights of Negroes in Mississippi or of the Uzbeks in Central Asia.

Sakharov advances another radical suggestion. He proposes to outlaw all 'export' of revolution by military or military-economic means – that is the kind of 'revolutions' imposed upon eastern Europe by the Soviet armed forces at the end of World War II. At the same time he would outlaw 'counter-revolutions' of the same type, that is, for example, the kind of operation the United States mounted against Cuba at the time of the Bay of Pigs or the imposition by the United States of the present economic sanctions against Communist China.

It has been 'official' Soviet doctrine since the time of Lenin that Communists do not believe in the 'export' of revolution – even though for many years Moscow supported the Comintern, an international organization dedicated to bringing about revolutions in all countries of the world. What is radical and innovatory in Sakharov's proposal is his substitution of the 'rights of man' thesis for the 'just and unjust wars' theory, under which the Soviet Union has classically reserved to itself the right to intervene on the side of colonial peoples struggling to liberate themselves from imperial powers or right-wing dictatorships anywhere in the world.

Sakharov suggests that his formulation would create conditions which would provide an opportunity to prevent such right-wing military coups as those in Greece and Indonesia.

He obviously does not believe that the 'rights of man' formulation would eliminate all wars, nor all wars arising from liberation movements, for he specifically states that 'with the elimination of all doubtful cases it would be easier to take decisive action in those extreme cases of reaction, racism, and militarism that allow no course other than armed struggle.' While he does not spell out his thoughts specifically, he leaves the strong implication here and elsewhere that Communist China might provide one of the 'extreme cases' he has in mind. South Africa might be another. A new military adventure by the United States in Cuba might be a third. But there is a clear implication that Sakharov's military intervention would be carried forward only under the flag of the United Nations. In essence, what he seems to propose is a kind of United Nations Korean policy, turned inside out; a mustering of the moral authority and *military force* of the United Nations against nations which are citadels of reaction and injustice.

8. Sakharov's analysis of the impending world food crisis closely follows that of American population and food specialists. Possibly his date of 1975–80 for the projected world food crisis is a little earlier than that projected by some American experts – but not much. He directs the thrust of his social criticism equally at the two superpowers, Russia and the United States, and advances the criticism often heard in the United States with respect to Vietnam policy – so long as the superpowers devote so huge a percentage of their national incomes to arms production and military competition, no real progress can be expected in solving social-economic ills.

He makes two interesting points: one is that unless Russia and Communism take leadership of the fight against hunger, the coming crisis will impose upon future generations a cynical and anti-Communist mark. Here he would appear to be offering an oblique criticism of Soviet policy towards underdeveloped nations. Soviet policy in this respect has been, largely, a carbon copy of American policy. Russia has sponsored aid and development programmes in Asian nations, alongside those of the United States. Both nations basically have used aid as an element in power politics to win, say, the favour of India, by assisting her in economic and social developments.

Neither the United States nor Russia has been notably successful in winning friends and increasing influence by this means, and the Chinese Communists have effectively raised the cry against Russia in Asia that the Soviet interest is, in essence, just that of another great power. The same cry has been raised by Fidel Castro and the Cubans against Soviet policy in Latin America where, the Cubans insist, the Russians have been as interested as the Americans in maintaining the *status quo* and dealing with the existing military power structures on a brokerage basis.

Sakharov calls for a radically new approach to the whole question. He attacks the United States and Americans for their failure to allocate sufficient resources to begin to lift the economic and social levels of citizens in depressed areas of the world, including black America. He believes that the American investment in backward areas must be raised to levels which would seriously curtail American economic growth – a sacrifice which he would justify for the sake of preserving mankind and for the lofty goal of preventing the destruction of world civilization. He calls for similar though not quite so drastic (their standard of living is not so high) sacrifices by Russia and the other developed nations in order to produce a dramatic and sudden rise in the standard of living of backward countries. He proposes a tax equal to twenty per cent of the national incomes of all developed nations for this purpose.

There is no doubt that investment on this kind of magnitude would make an impact on the depressed and backward countries. It would also, as Sakharov indicates, radically limit the ability of the superpowers to continue their present high-level arms investments.

It is not entirely clear exactly what Sakharov means by 'national income'. Does he mean the national budget? This would mean an annual investment of nearly $35 billion for the United States, based on the 1968 annual budget of about $170 billion. The Soviet contribution, based on a budget of roughly 123.6 billion roubles would be close to $30 billion.

If Sakharov literally means that the United States should contribute twenty per cent of its national income or gross national product this would be quite another thing. The total United States income figure in 1968 was about $800 billion so this would mean an aid total in the range of $140 to $160 billion. Soviet income is estimated at about half that of the United States, which would make their total $70 to $80 billion.

These figures come close to doubling the budget of each country. However, if the United States and the Soviet Union were able to arrive at an arms holiday the net weight of aid to less advanced countries would be measurably lightened. The total United States military budget now runs in the neighbourhood of $70 to $80 billion.

Sakharov indicates that the Americans should overcome what he calls the present unwillingness of 'white citizens ... to accept even minimum sacrifices to eliminate the unequal economic and cultural position of the country's black citizens, who make up ten per cent of the population'.

Numerous American proposals have been advanced for annual investment of up to $15 or $20 billion a year for the problems of the cities and the urban minorities. These have generally been conditioned upon the ending of the Vietnam war and the application of the $20 to $30 billion now being spent for the war to domestic racial and poverty programmes.

The economic suggestions by Sakharov suggest some gaps in his knowledge of economic and budgetary matters as well as a less than precise knowledge of the general state of United States racial relations, the efforts by large and important groups of white Americans to obtain effective action to improve the status of blacks and, perhaps more significantly, the effects of the programme which he advocates upon American economy.

Sakharov believes that American investments of the magnitude he suggests in deprived areas of the world would automatically curtail the United States rate of economic growth. In fact, such a programme might well produce precisely the opposite effect as American facilities were expanded to produce more and more goods, machinery, and food for supply to backward regions, and as larger and larger use was made of American productive facilities with a resultant increase in employment and rise in domestic living standards. The programme proposed by Sakharov might well touch off the greatest economic boom in American (and world) history.

9. Only within the last half dozen years have questions of conservation of national resources and pollution begun to receive public attention in the Soviet Union. Until that time the attitude in Russia resembled that of mid-nineteenth century America. Russia was a land of such enormous wealth, such inexhaustible resources of forest, water, soil, metals, and minerals, that any serious diminution or despoliation seemed unthinkable. As recently as ten years ago it was possible to fly across the Siberian taiga and witness forest fires burning over thousands of square miles with no one paying the slightest attention. Siberian settlers, like their counterparts on the American frontier, habitually fired the forest to clear land for the plough. Even today the Russian husbandman thinks nothing of cutting 100-year-old pines and spruce, transforming the magnificent trees into timber with an axe in order to build a cabin or cowshed. Most Russian peasant izbas outside the Ukraine are still built with the traditional, and wasteful, logs. No coherent or coordinated system of forest management, forest renewal, or forest conservation is in effect in the whole country.

Wildlife, game, bird, and fish resources have seemed so

stupendous that no effort has been made to curtail hunting or fishing or to protect species. The sturgeon of the Volga and the Caspian have been seined so vigorously that caviare, once as common as peanut butter and as cheap, is moving towards the vanishing point. The situation is compounded by massive pollution of the lower Volga and the Caspian by oil refineries, oil tankers, and oil barges. The Caspian is rapidly becoming too saline to support fish or other life but no comprehensive effort has been made to regenerate or protect this invaluable inland sea. The Volga has been transformed into a succession of lakes behind vast hydro-electric dams, and the lakes are turning into cesspools of pollution and sedimentation.

One of the enormous projects of Stalin's late years was the so-called Kakhovka hydroelectric and water conservancy project. This was a scheme to impound waters in the arid south Ukraine, an attempt to generate electric power and irrigate thousands of square miles of semi-desert. Stalin's engineers – all in the employ of Lavrenti P. Beria's police – conceived the notion of creating a vast lake which, in addition to serving as a reservoir for the hydroelectric and irrigation system, would influence and modify the climate of the whole region. It was a grandiose scheme but it did not work. It salinated huge areas of crop lands, and the lake has become a dismal swamp filled with fetid and rotting vegetation – a pestilent area so noisome that even airplane pilots avoid flying over it.

The most notorious case of pollution, however, is that of Lake Baikal. This unique lake in eastern Siberia is more than a mile deep and nearly four hundred miles long. It is so great that it holds nearly one-fifth of all the world's fresh-lake water. Baikal lies in a north-south crevasse in the earth's crust. It is 25,000,000 years old and has hardly changed in that period. More than 1,000 species of plants, shellfish, fish, and animals are found there and in no other place in the world. The lake's water is of remarkable purity, so free of dissolved minerals that anyone drowned there quickly vanishes completely – tiny crustaceans eat the flesh and the skeleton dissolves in the pure water.

Despite the uniqueness of the lake, despite its remarkable role as a laboratory for forms of life found nowhere else, a worldwide campaign to save it from pollution has failed. An enormous wood pulp complex has been set up at Baikalsk on the south shore which is pouring into the lake quantities of sulphurous wastes, poisoning the waters, and raising their temperature. Baikal has been lost, just as have so many of America's lakes and rivers.

Smog and air pollution are not yet a major problem in the great Soviet cities, largely because the automobile has not yet become so prominent on the Soviet landscape. But current Soviet planning provides for mass production of automobiles, 1,000,000 or more yearly, beginning in the 1970s. Smog and auto congestion lie just ahead. Meantime, Soviet industrial centres in the Urals and Siberia and the Ukraine remind the visitor of old-fashioned Pittsburgh – mills pour masses of soot-laden smoke and chemical pollutants into the sky with no hindrance from municipal authorities.

10. The point made by Sakharov regarding police dictatorships is one which may seem more dramatic to his Soviet readers than to Americans – this is his equation of Hitlerism and Stalinism as two variants of the same basic tyranny. Soviet official statements always make clear distinction between the villainy of Hitler and what is described as the more limited (and semi-justified) villainy of Stalin. Many ordinary Russians accept this view. Sakharov, however, draws no essential distinction between Hitler, Stalin, and Mao; between anti-Semitism under Hitler and anti-Semitism under Stalin; between Hitler's myth of the inevitable war in the East and Stalin's claim that the longer the Soviet state existed the sharper the class struggle; between the cult of Stalin and that of Mao; between German *lebensraum* and Chinese *lebensraum*; between Hitler's

book-burning and Mao's anti-intellectualism; between Nazi stormtroopers and the Red Guards; between Eichmann and Himmler and the Soviet Police Chiefs Yezhov and Beria.

The cliché of Soviet propaganda has always been that Hitler was encouraged in his rise by German capitalists and international monopolies in which the United States participated. Sakharov pays nominal heed to this concept but makes a far more critical point, one often touched upon in the West but seldom, even now, mentioned in Russia. This was Stalin's open culpability for Hitler's rise because Stalin insisted that the German Communists make the German Social Democrats, rather than Hitler's Nazis, their chief enemy. The role of Stalin in advocating policies which directly led to the debacle which brought Hitler into power has been well documented by Ruth Fischer in her famous book, *Stalin and German Communism*. Sakharov cites a letter by Ernst Henri, an *émigré* German Communist, to Ilya Ehrenburg in which Henri details the disastrous effects of Stalin's insistence that the German Communists under no circumstances should form a united front with the Social Democrats against Hitler. Actually, had the Communists and Social Democrats joined forces they could easily have defeated the Nazis, who came into power on a minority vote, achieved only because of the disunity on the left. Stalin considered the Social Democrats 'Social Fascists'. He affected to believe that with the destruction of the German Social Democrats, Communism could easily cope with Hitler. The result is history.

11. Sakharov evaluates Stalin as a more dangerous tyrant than Hitler because, while Hitler was open in his demagoguery and evil, Stalin concealed his under a hypocritical mask of pseudo-popular Socialist ideology.

The most savage blows of Stalin's tyranny, Sakharov believes, fell on the Soviet working men and women, the very class which had brought the Communists into power, the proletariat in whose name the Bolsheviks made the revolution.

Sakharov offers an estimate for the death toll of the Stalinist camps which accords strikingly with the estimates of David Dallin, the Russian Menshevik and profoundly anti-Communist scholar whose studies of Stalin's concentration camp system in the 1940s and 1950s were considered by many objective Westerners to err on the side of exaggeration.

Sakharov's estimate of 10 to 15 million deaths in the camps in exile and by execution still seems high. But it accords with the guesses of many Russians who survived the camps. The famous Soviet author Aleksandr Solzhenitsyn, a prison camp victim and a man who has made an intimate study of the system, presents estimates quite similar to Sakharov's.

Sakharov adopts another attitude which will shock many Soviet readers – but not so many foreigners. He calls Stalin's camps the prototypes of the Hitler death camps. The same analogy has been drawn by Solzhenitsyn.

Sakharov mentions the deaths of prisoners in labour camps in Norilsk, a mining and metallurgical centre in the Soviet north, and Vorkuta, an enormous northern coal-mining complex where the first labour camp riots broke out in 1954 after Stalin's death. He talks of the 'death ships' in the Sea of Okhotsk in the Soviet Far East, a subject vividly dealt with by Evgenia Ginsburg in her *Into the Whirlwind*. Madame Ginsburg was a prisoner on one of these ships and her life was spared only by a fluke.

Stalin ordered the Tatars deported from their Crimean homeland at the end of the war because of a suspicion (accurate) that many collaborated with the Nazis during the war. The action involved the removal of hundreds of thousands of families. They were sent to Central Asia and Siberia where large numbers perished of cold and starvation. Only within most recent years have the Crimean

Tatars been officially 'rehabilitated', that is, declared guilty of no crime and victims of unjust persecution. Why their rehabilitation was delayed until fifteen years after Stalin's death no one knows, unless possibly Khrushchev had some hand in the original crime and therefore was reluctant to right the wrong. Many other nationalities were subjected to similar arbitrary deportation. The Volga Germans, settlers who had been brought into the Volga region and the Ukraine by Catherine the Great in the late eighteenth century, were sent to Central Asia and the Arctic at the beginning of World War II in fear they might provide a fifth column for Hitler. Only within recent years have a few been permitted to return to their Volga and Ukraine countryside. The Kalmyks, a Mongol tribe of the Volga region, were deported both before and after the war; so were half a dozen small mountain nationalities in the Caucasus. Disloyalty, collaboration with Hitler: these were the standard charges. Tens of thousands were deported from the Baltic states at the end of World War II. Stalin, according to Khrushchev, wanted to deport the whole of the Ukraine to Siberia but was dissuaded on grounds that there wasn't room for them all in the East. At the time of his death in 1953, Stalin apparently was contemplating shipping all of Russia's surviving Jews (about 3.5 million) to Siberia. The plan was aborted by his sudden death, 5 March 1953.

12. One of Stalin's most remarkable aberrations was a blind faith in the pact which he signed with Hitler in August 1939. In 1937–8 in the most savage of his purges he had wiped out not only the whole high command of the Red Army and thousands of his top industrial and party chiefs but had methodically executed or imprisoned almost every officer in the Soviet armed forces down to and including division commanders. The purge was so devastating that in some military districts the highest surviving officer was a major or lieutenant-colonel. Between one-third and

one-half of the 75,000 officers in the Red Army were shot or imprisoned.

With his armed forces in a state of shock from this blood-letting, Stalin broke off negotiations in mid-summer, 1939, with the British and French for a common front against Hitler and signed, instead, a non-aggression pact with his most deadly enemy. Less than a year later Hitler began his long, careful, and inevitably not-very-secret preparations for war against the Soviet Union. Stalin's intelligence was excellent. Hundreds of espionage reports of the most detailed kind poured in to the Kremlin about the German preparations for attack on the Soviet Union. Warnings came to him from the United States and Winston Churchill. He declined to heed any of the reports, attributing them to a British plot to drag him into the war. Only at the last possible moment did he much too belatedly permit the most elementary precautions to be taken. When the Nazis attacked at 4 a.m., 22 June, the Soviet Union was in a state of general unpreparedness. Even after the German attack began Stalin refused to credit it. Hours after the Nazi bombers were blasting Soviet cities and Nazi panzers were ripping deep into the Soviet soil, Stalin still believed it was a mistake, a provocation by Hitler's generals, not by his trusted colleague, the Fuehrer himself.

Aleksandr M. Nekrich, a respected Soviet historian, has pieced together the story of the events leading up to the German attack on 22 June; the massive intelligence warnings; the persistent ignoring of the storm signals; the fatal mistakes in disposition of defence forces; the terrible cost to the Soviet armed forces and to the Soviet people. His book was published in 1965 and won high critical praise. Then, with an intensification of ideological warfare on the part of neo-Stalinists, Nekrich was savagely attacked in 1967 and expelled from the Communist party. His thesis, however, is generally accepted within the Soviet Union. The attacks on Nekrich are generally regarded as having been inspired by neo-Stalinist elements in the armed forces propaganda apparatus and possibly by neo-Stalinists in the Soviet High Command.

Many other Soviet historians have dealt in part with this subject; it was touched upon extensively by Khrushchev in his 'secret speech', in which he depicted Stalin as having failed to heed the mass of evidence that poured in to him and to have, as a result, suffered a kind of nervous breakdown on 22 June when it finally penetrated his consciousness that Hitler had betrayed him.

Sakharov refers to 'the notes of Major General Grigorenko', which he presumably has read in manuscript or mimeograph form since they have not been permitted to be published in the Soviet Union and are not known outside of Russia.

Major General Pyotr G. Grigorenko was a major-general in World War II and saw distinguished service. After the war he became a cybernetics specialist in the Frunze Military Academy until he lost his job in 1961 after writing a letter of protest to Premier Khrushchev about discrimination against Jews in the Soviet Army. Three years later he was stripped of his rank and lost his pension because of an accusation that he had made anti-Soviet speeches. Grigorenko, like many dissidents of recent years, was sent to a mental institution. He was confined there until 1966 when he was released. He obtained a menial job in a Soviet supply organization but did not give up his fight for civil rights in the Soviet Union. He has been prominent in the fight of Soviet writers for freedom of publication and joined with writers and other Soviet dissidents in vigorous manifestations and protests over the trial of four young Russian writers in January 1968, who were charged with anti-Soviet activity. Grigorenko and his fellow dissidents charged that the trial violated all norms of Soviet legality.

13. No extensive analysis of Stalin's repressive policy in Soviet agriculture has yet been published although Nikita Khrushchev often vividly criticized certain aspects of it.

The policy was characterized by the forced organization of the peasantry into collectives (largely accomplished at gun-point and by driving hundreds of thousands of richer, more successful peasants off the land into Siberian labour); the imposition of arbitrary quotas for grain and foodstuffs delivery at fixed low prices to the state; an income system which held the peasants at a subsistence level; the anchoring of peasants to the land through a kind of forced indenture system (they were not permitted to acquire the internal passports without which movement from country to city was illegal); the monopolization of farm machinery and particularly tractors in 'machine tractor stations' which provided services to the peasant farmers at prices and under conditions controlled by Moscow; the imposition upon the 'collective' farms of chairmen or bosses, selected by the Communist party, either locally or in Moscow, with the primary assignment of producing food for the city, regardless of consequences; or as Sakharov insists 'on a basis of cunning and obsequiousness' – ability to fool and please the higher authorities.

The net result of Stalin's policies was that in 1953, after he was dead, it was discovered that the pool of Soviet livestock and farm animals was about the same size as it had been in 1916, the last full Tsarist year; grain production had hardly grown in twenty years and was roughly on the levels of the pre-collectivization days of the late 1920s. Stalin, in Khrushchev's words, had not seen the countryside since the early 1930s and presumed that conditions there were those depicted for him in rosy-tinted Soviet movies.

14. Stalin's police sent to prison camps and exile almost every Soviet man and woman who survived capture by the Germans and the Nazi camps and labour system. Most of them were herded into prison trains and sent directly from the barbed-wire enclosures of the Third Reich to the barbed-wire enclosures of eastern Siberia. Soviet soldiers who fell into German hands and managed to escape back

to their own lines met an even more terrible fate. They were shot as spies or sent into penalty battalions for front-line service in tasks almost certain to bring death.

The 'anti-worker' decrees mentioned by Sakharov were an elaborate system of penal laws under which Soviet workers were virtual prisoners, unable to leave their employment or shift to another job under penalty of imprisonment. They were subject to penal deprivation for unauthorized absence, lateness, poor quality work, and infractions of discipline. Damage to equipment or ordinary mistakes in production could be equated with sabotage under a special Soviet legal concept of 'analogy', by which an act for which no criminal penalty was prescribed could be punished as being 'analogous to treason', etc.

The exile of 'entire peoples' concerned the Crimean Tatars, Volga Germans, Caucasian mountain tribes, and smaller nationality groups, such as Greek settlers who had been scattered around the shores of the Black Sea since the time of Jason and the Golden Fleece.

Anti-Semitism was endemic in the Soviet police apparatus and in Stalin's personal attitudes. It became manifest in the early 1930s and steadily deepened with the years. By the end of the Stalin epoch, Jews were systematically excluded from all major government posts and specifically from the High Command, the Foreign Office, the higher ranks of the party, and other responsible areas (with a handful of exceptions). Quotas had been imposed for Jews in the universities, and Jewish faculty members had been rooted out of many institutes and institutions of higher learning.

Stalin was equally hostile and suspicious of Ukranians and, as Khrushchev revealed, toyed with the idea of exiling them all to Siberia. This hostility probably dated to the days of the Civil War in 1918–21 or possibly even earlier and may have had its origin in a kind of super-Great Russian chauvinism which was characteristic of Stalin even though he himself was a Georgian by birth.

The imposition of harsh penalties for trivial or nonexistent offences was characteristic of the Stalin police empire. The industrial department of the police was constantly searching for new categories of 'prisoners' in order to replenish the labour force of Siberia, which was extraordinarily large and extraordinarily inefficient due to the slipshod management, cruelty, graft, corruption, sadism, and deprivations.

15. Nothing is known in the West of the 1,000-page monograph of R. Medvedev, analysing the origin and development of Stalinism. It is evident from Sakharov that this is a theoretical work, analysing Stalin from a Marxist viewpoint. From the fact that it has not yet been published within the Soviet Union it may be deduced that Medvedev does not accept the official thesis that Stalin's acts were a species of late aberration, a personal kind of flaw that developed in a man who originally was, and to some extent throughout his life continued to be, a dedicated and principled Marxist and disciple of Lenin. All official Soviet interpretations of Stalin have angrily rejected the implication that there was anything wrong with the Soviet system; that Stalin was in any way a product of the proletarian dictatorship and 'democratic centralism' (read: dictatorship by an oligarchy) foisted on the Bolshevik party in its struggling conspiratorial days by Lenin.

The contrary thesis, that Lenin by inventing a disciplined apparatus with tight control by one man or a small group of men; with a tradition of orders from top down to bottom; with unquestioned acceptance of a decision once it had been made, inevitably produced a dictator has been advanced by Yugoslav, Italian, and Western Marxist students.

It is probable that Medvedev's analysis reflects this viewpoint and that it is documented with detailed examples drawn from the actual process by which Stalin manipulated the party and used Lenin's principles of 'dictatorship of the proletariat', 'democratic centralism', and cellular organization to place himself in complete control of a state and maintain himself by the paranoid exercise of police power. Sakharov and Medvedev obviously are friendly controversialists as can be seen from Sakharov's reference. The reference to Medvedev suggests that Sakharov has discussed these problems extensively within the scientific-technological intelligentsia and that a considerable range of opinions exists within these circles.

16. Sakharov is well aware that his 'thoughts' are likely to be attacked by his comrades (he himself would appear to be a member of the Communist party) on grounds of deviation from Marxist purity or 'Westernism', as he calls it. This is a serious allegation in Soviet polemics, for it carries with it the implication of subservience to an alien, i.e., Western or antagonistic viewpoint and a reflection in some manner upon loyalty and ideological purity. Sakharov takes note of this line of criticism and builds a small defence by emphasizing his awareness that the Western world is not without its own special evils. But he suggests that his Soviet critics probably do not know as much about the evils of Western society as they think and certainly not as much as Western Communists who live, work, and struggle in a capitalist environment. In a word, Sakharov suggests, maybe there are some virtues in 'Western' views which Russian critics do not perceive. As for himself, he prefers to criticize what is immediately before him; the Soviet ills which he so well knows.

17. Unlike some Soviet intellectuals, Sakharov gives full credit to Khrushchev for starting the Soviet Union down the path of sweeping away the heritage of Stalinism. During Khrushchev's heyday many Soviet intellectuals and scientists of Sakharov's milieu were inclined to be contemptuous of Khrushchev for his crudities, his anti-intellectualism, his braggadocio, his egocentricity. They found this

embarrassing, and they also were disturbed and annoyed by his rambunctious forays into one field after the other, often fields in which he knew very little. For example, they welcomed his aid in eliminating Stalin's Science Tsar, Trofim Lysenko, but not Khrushchev's reconciliation with Lysenko (after Lysenko apparently persuaded Khrushchev he had found a short-cut to boost Soviet milk and butter production – by milking cows more frequently). They valued Khrushchev's efforts to cope with Russian agricultural problems but recognized for the gamble that it was Khrushchev's attempt to solve the grain deficit by ploughing the virgin (but arid) lands of Kazakhstan and southwest Siberia. They favoured Khrushchev's effort to increase Soviet corn production but not Khrushchev's endorsement of corn as the cure-all for Soviet farm problems or his naïve efforts to extend corn north to the Moscow region (the equivalent, latitudinally, of Labrador).

What Sakharov calls 'Khrushchev's mistakes of a voluntarist character' refers to Khrushchev's penchant for ill-judged, personal interventions. By 'voluntarist' Sakharov means unprincipled, illogical adventurist policy – quite possibly the Cuban missile crisis and similar Khrushchevisms.

The fact that Khrushchev inevitably bore responsibility for Stalin's crimes along with most of his colleagues has been one of the unmentioned subjects of the post-Stalin years. Indeed, when Khrushchev delivered his famous 'secret speech' in 1956 he was said to have been interrupted from the floor by a questioner who demanded: 'Where were you when this was going on?' To which Khrushchev replied that he was right there, just as frightened as all the rest, powerless to do anything to halt Stalin's headlong course.

18. The demand that the exposure of Stalin's crimes be carried out more completely has been heard repeatedly since 1956. The exposures by Khrushchev were devastating but partial. They were, in effect, largely limited to Stalin's

later years from 1938 onwards, touching only lightly on the first purge trials, the so-called Yagoda period. Khrushchev came down most heavily on Stalin's late period and the participation of Stalin's last Police Chief, Lavrenti P. Beria.

The post-Stalin regime has painstakingly combed the records and released hundreds of thousands from prison camps. It has carried out the posthumous 'rehabilitation' of thousands of prisoners. However, the full records of the N.K.V.D. and its predecessor police agencies have not been opened up; indeed, they are tightly closed except to the private and secret party investigatory commissions.

Nothing has ever been released indicating the relationship of Stalin to crimes and purges in other countries, although it is known that he exterminated almost the entire leadership of the Polish Communist party before World War II, as well as important segments of the Hungarian, German, Finnish, and indeed almost any exiled Communist groups who had had the ill chance to be in the Soviet Union. Evidence suggesting a Soviet role in the death of Jan Masaryk and other crimes in Czechoslovakia has only begun to be brought to light – but in Prague and not in Moscow.

Many other matters have been only lightly touched upon; the nature of the so-called Leningrad Affair, in which Stalin executed the party leaders of Leningrad in 1949 and 1950, has never been disclosed. Khrushchev hinted that Stalin was responsible for the death of Sergei Kirov, the Leningrad party leader whose murder in 1934 was used as an excuse for a whole decade of purges and executions but nothing has been published of the inquiry which Khrushchev said must be made. There has been no reopening of the 'cases' against Kamenev, Zinoviev, the complex charges against Trotsky, and many others.

Sakharov's revelation that in 1964 it was planned symbolically to expel Stalin from the party and publicly rehabilitate his victims had not previously been known. Presumably this action was to have been carried out as a postscript to the removal of Stalin's body from the mausoleum where he rested for eight years beside Lenin.

Sakharov's estimate that one half of the party membership was arrested between 1936–9 also never before has been made public; nor his revelation that 600,000 party members were shot in this period and that only 50,000 of the 1.2 million taken into custody regained their freedom. Khrushchev in his famous secret speech is the authority for the Stalinist toll in the higher echelons of the party. In the same period, he revealed, Stalin arrested 1,108 of the 1,966 delegates to the 1934 Party Congress (the so-called 'Congress of Victors') and ninety-eight out of 139 members of the Party Central Committee. Almost all of these men and women were shot.

19. There is hardly a more sensitive political subject in the Soviet Union than that of the role of the neo-Stalinists. This refers to those bureaucrats, party leaders, factory managers, writers, and other elements of Soviet society who seek to reimpose upon the country the kind of tough, police-backed, authoritarian, narrow-minded, anti-intellectual, anti-foreign, chauvinistic, and paranoid style of society characteristic of the Stalin era. Many of these individuals came to power under Stalin. Many of these sincerely believe that Stalin's way is the only way in which so vast and naturally disorderly and diverse a conglomeration as the 230,000,000 Soviet people can be governed. Many know no other way of governing except by the use of threat, force, and fear. They have no experience in participatory management. The tradition of edict and decree, it must be remembered, was strong and characteristic of pre-revolutionary Russia and in many respects the tradition was taken over virtually unchanged, intensified by the Bolsheviks and reinforced by Stalin. It is this group and the Soviet Military which played the leading role in the Soviet action in Czechoslovakia.

Sakharov's reference to 'anti-Leninist pseudo-socialism' and the rise in the Soviet Union of 'a distinct class – a bureaucratic elite from which all key positions are filled and which is rewarded for its work through open and concealed privileges' comes close to being an accurate description of Soviet bureaucratic elitism and reflects the famous views of Milovan Djilas whose work, *The New Class*, analysing the rise of a bureaucratic elite in Yugoslavia caused him to be imprisoned for many years by Marshal Tito (he is now once again at liberty). Sakharov apparently believes that the New Class concept provides only a partial explanation of neo-Stalinism.

Soviet officialdom is intensely self-conscious of the charge of neo-Stalinism. This writer has seldom been so sharply rebuked by Soviet officials as for his repeated assertion that there has risen in Russia in the last decade a powerful grouping of neo-Stalinist forces, comprising in part top-echelon political leaders, in part young ambitious party leaders who seek to advance through the influence of police terrorism, in part traditionalist managers who simply do not know how to govern or accomplish their industrial or agricultural tasks except through the use of arbitrary force, and in part of debased intelligentsia, writers, editors, painters, musicians, who have been subverted by power, position, prestige, and privilege.

20. Sergei P. Trapeznikov is a close and long-time associate of Party Secretary Brezhnev. He emerged in a position of influence in Moldavia when Brezhnev was first secretary of the Moldavian Communist Party before being brought into Moscow as one of Khrushchev's chief lieutenants. Trapeznikov was a typical provincial party propagandist, occupying the post of director of the Higher Party School in Kishinev, a training institution for ideology and party doctrine. He came up to Moscow when Brezhnev began to rise in the central apparatus and was placed by

Brezhnev on the editorial board of the party's journal, *Questions of History of the Communist Party,* an organ of the Central Committee Institute of Marxism-Leninism.

Trapeznikov is an agricultural specialist. He won an award of the Red Banner of Labour for 'agricultural successes' in Moldavia, and most of his published writings deal with agricultural, economic and organizational questions. He holds a degree as a Doctor of Historical Science and was nominated as a candidate for corresponding membership (the lowest rank) in the Soviet Academy of Sciences, history department, in 1964. He was placed at the head of the Party Central Committee Department of Sciences and Educational Institutions in late 1965. This was a new Central Committee organ, not previously existing.

His published writings firmly identify Trapeznikov as a conservative of strong neo-Stalinist orientation. One of his first *Pravda* articles after assuming his Central Committee role in 1965 contained a thinly veiled call for substantial rehabilitation of Stalin and harshly attacked anti-Stalinism and the liberal segment of Soviet opinion.

There were some signs in late 1967 that Trapeznikov had lost his post (possibly as a result of the obvious antagonism in Soviet scientific circles to an official of such Stalinist orientation) but in 1968 he continued to publish articles in the agricultural sphere which strongly veer back towards Stalinist practices, towards increasing state control over peasant farm management, and even towards some Maoist-Chinese concepts of Commune agriculture.

It is hardly likely that an individual of such tendencies, even though he is 'unquestionably intelligent, shrewd and highly consistent', in Sakharov's words, would find common ground with the 'scientific and scientific-technological intelligentsia.' Apparently Trapeznikov was turned down by a membership vote of the Academy of Sciences but in spite of this fact was continued in his party supervisory role by the Brezhnev–Kosygin leadership.

21. Sakharov's attack on Mao, the Chinese Communists, and the 'crimes of the Maoists' against human rights is couched in terms so strong as to support the conclusion that he favours military intervention by 'the world's democratic forces', presumably under the banner of the United Nations, in protection of the 'rights of man' in Communist China. In his view, the depredations of Mao and his associates are far more critical than the 'imperialist peril' in Africa, Latin America, or the Middle East. He would seem to regard the situation in China as possibly the most grave of any in the world today – a view which is supported by large numbers of his countrymen, both party and non-party.

In rejecting any idea of restoration of the 'unity' of the Communist world, Sakharov takes the view that the split between China and the Soviet-led Communist movement is, in fact, a split between Communists and non-Communists (he regards the Chinese as a non-Communist group), hence talk of unity is illusory and foolish; he rejects unity between Communists and non-Communists in such conditions as a contradiction in terms. In other words, he views the break between Moscow and Peking as a logical development in the conflicting evolution of Russian and Chinese policy. Because of the seriousness of the 'disease', he sees the split as a means of quarantine. It should be noted that the Chinese take a parallel view of the division in the Communist world. *They* see Moscow as the deviationist group and hold that Moscow has abandoned Communism and that the true faith is to be found only in Peking. They, too, see no point in unity between Communists (Peking) and the apostasy (Moscow).

22. Sakharov cites four general tendencies which threaten the integrity of the personality, one of which is found principally in the West, one in the Soviet Union, and two in both cultures.

The first is what he calls 'mass culture' – the stupefying

impact of television, radio, advertising commercials, style, faddism, materialistic values, and standards which suppress or extinguish personality by a general lowering of intellectual standards, motivational objectives, and multiple stimuli.

The second is authoritarianism in education. He grants the virtues of an educational system controlled by government rather than church and the value of universal education. But he warns against excessive centralization, standardization, authoritarianism, limitation of discussion, and intellectual challenge which, he suggests, is similar to the Mandarin system of education in old China and to its establishment of Confucianism as a virtual canon body. He is echoing familiar criticisms of the Soviet educational system with its emphasis on a centrally imposed curriculum, rote learning, and suppression of intellectual adventurism.

The third threat, in his opinion, arises from chemical and mechanical control of life processes – birth-control techniques, the employment of tranquillizers, narcotics, depressants, stimulants, and other chemicals to affect personality and response, the potential of affecting conduct through electrodes inserted in the brain (experimentation with such techniques in laboratory animals has been carried out both in the United States and the Soviet Union), and other artificial methods of directing or influencing mass behaviour. He includes in this category, apparently, the use of advertising and propaganda methods.

The fourth threat he sees is man's increased reliance upon mechanical means of decision-making, the use of computers to determine priorities or to select optimum goals or paths toward goals. He points to the warning by Norbert Wiener that it is impossible to programme machines to respond like normal human beings with all the human conflicts and irrationalities. The programming must, by its nature, follow patterns of logic and hence produces the danger that human beings, by reliance upon electronic automatism, may lose control over their destiny.

23. In the final weeks of his intellectual life in 1922–3 before a fatal series of cerebral haemorrhages deprived him of the ability to think and act, Lenin was concentrating his attention upon the bureaucratic and other evils of the system of government which was largely his creation. He had begun to perceive its essentially arbitrary and manipulative nature as well as the perils which were becoming apparent from Stalin's ambitious ruthlessness. In the early Bolshevik era, Lenin had inclined to the view that any cook, as Sakharov notes, could quickly learn to govern. Lenin said that a clerk could learn the secret of running a bank in a week. He pooh-poohed expertise and the value of experience in conducting the affairs of state. But in his twilight hours, he began to see that he had created a massive robot state, insensitive to the people whom it governed, responsive to the individual who sat at the controls, faithfully fulfilling orders regardless of what they were.

In the mechanistic Soviet structure as shown in Czechoslovakia, the role of censorship is central since it serves simultaneously to conceal from both the rulers and the ruled any deviations from the expressed line of conduct and is capable of suppressing any facts which challenge the central theses of decisions or policy. Thus, for example, in conditions of Soviet censorship it was impossible in the months before Hitler's attack on Russia on 22 June 1941, for those who believed such an attack to be impending to place any warnings before the public so long as Stalin adhered to the doctrine that the Germans were not preparing to attack. In the face of such a dictum by Stalin, to assert the contrary was tantamount to treason. The whole apparatus of the state censorship made certain that no hint of anything other than Stalin's official line was presented to the public.

Sakharov cites the American sociologist Lewis A. Coser to support his view of the viciousness of censorship and the role which it plays in the alienation of progressive and avant-garde authors of the West from the society in which they live.

Coser, in fact, in his book, *Men of Ideas, a Sociologist's View,* was discussing the censorship in the United States directed against so-called obscenity or words declared by the courts to be 'obscene, lewd or lascivious', the phenomenon of sexual censorship and the use of the censor to impose upon society the supposed moral standards of a middle-class puritanical society. Coser concluded that the censors inadvertently helped to bring about an alliance of diverse interests which in the end caused the downfall of the middle-class standards of morality.

24. Sakharov does not go so far as to suggest that Soviet censorship will produce the downfall of what it is intended to protect (the right of the dictatorial government to control the ideas and thinking of the Soviet people) but he emphasizes the debilitating effect of the censorship on Soviet literature and on Soviet creative thinking.

He cites the appeal of Aleksandr Solzhenitsyn for the removal of Soviet censorship. Solzhenitsyn's plea was submitted to the Praesidium of the Union of Soviet Writers on 16 May 1967, on the eve of the fourth National Congress of Soviet Writers.

Solzhenitsyn charged that for years an illegal censorship had been imposed in the Soviet Union by an agency known as Glavlit (Chief Literary Administration) which held all literary productions under strict control. He contended that Glavlit is a violation of the Soviet constitution.

Under the aegis of Glavlit not a single novel, play, short story, poem, or work of nonfiction may be published in Russia without Glavlit's official stamp. Even the text of matchbox covers and restaurant menus must bear a Glavlit permit number.

Because of Glavlit's pervasiveness, Solzhenitsyn charged, magazines and publishing houses often reject manuscripts out of hand, simply because the editor feels the work would not win Glavlit approval. Equally serious, Solzhenitsyn charged, was the practice of imposing changes and revisions on authors in order to get Glavlit approval.

Solzhenitsyn called on the Union of Soviet Writers to demand abolition of the illegal censorship and to begin to defend writers and creative freedom instead of acting as an arm of the state in imposing unconstitutional controls.

He cited a long list of writers who had been subjected to suppression, persecution, imprisonment, and execution under the Soviet regime. More than six hundred writers, he contended, had been handed over into Stalinist camps without protest by the Union, and often the Union had eagerly joined in the persecution. His list of writers who had been persecuted or who had died under Stalinist terror included Anna Akhmatova, Isaak Babel, Mikhail Bulgakov, Ivan Bunin, Aleksandr Grin, Vasily Grossman, Nikolai Gumilev, Nikolai Klyuyev, Osip Mandelshtam, Vladimir Mayakovsky, Boris Pasternak, Boris Pilnyak, Andrei Platonov, Aleksei Remizov, Titian Tabidze, Marina Tsvetayeva, Artem Vesely, Pavel Vasilycv, Maximilian Voloshin, Sergei Yesenin, Yevgeny Zamyatin, Nikolai Zabolotsky, and Mikhail Zoshchenko.

Solzhenitsyn called on the Congress to demand the abolition of censorship, overt or hidden, of all fictional writing and the release of publishing houses from the obligation of obtaining prior authorization for the publication of every printed page.

Solzhenitsyn's proposals were not acted upon by the Congress. Instead, they led to a campaign of abuse and denunciation, subjecting Solzhenitsyn to allegations of treason, insanity, egoism, and persecution mania.

Solzhenitsyn has himself been one of the principal victims of the censorship. Two major novels, *The Cancer Ward* and *The First Circle*, have not been permitted to be published in the Soviet Union, although both have appeared in the West. Several of his plays and film scripts and many of his short stories have not seen the light of day. The secret police have repeatedly searched his residence, seizing his manuscripts and private papers.

25. Article 190 of the Criminal Code of the Russian Federated Soviet Republic concerns failure to report crimes and assesses penalties for such failure. Under the notorious Soviet legal doctrine of 'analogy', a person who fails to report a crime may be prosecuted and punished as severely as the person who commits the actual crime. Following widespread agitation and protest among Soviet writers and intellectuals against violations of Soviet Constitutional guarantees in the Galanskov–Ginzburg case of January 1968, the Supreme Soviet of the R.S.F.S.R. amended Article 190 to include within its penalties 'literary protests'. Thus, under the revised code, a person who knew of a literary protest which the courts judged to be a violation of the law was rendered subject to conviction if he did not report his knowledge to the public prosecutor. This amendment, in Sakharov's view, contravenes the Soviet Constitution's Bill of Rights.

26. The trial in 1966, of the Soviet authors Yuli M. Daniel and Andrei D. Sinyavsky on charges of smuggling out of the Soviet Union literary works which allegedly slandered the Soviet state, drew widespread protest within and outside Russia. Works of the two writers had been published abroad under *noms de plume*. They were convicted of 'anti-Soviet agitation' and given long labour camp sentences. The conviction of the men was protested against by writers of all political faiths, including Louis Aragon, a leading French Communist writer and intellectual, and Graham Greene, a British writer held in high Soviet regard. Agitation for the release and pardon of the two men has continued since their imprisonment. Mrs Daniel has been especially vigorous in her efforts to draw the attention of the intellectual world to the plight of her husband, who is in poor health and who has been subject to

harsh treatment. Despite the agitation, the men remain in prison.

27. Prison camps in Russia since the Stalin–Beria days have notably improved, but they are still far from convalescent homes. Sakharov's report on the locale in which political prisoners are now being held places them in the Mordvinian Republic, a remote, backward area west of the Middle Volga seldom if ever accessible to non-Russians. It is not clear from Sakharov's reference how many of the 50,000 prisoners in the Mordvinian area are 'politicals'. The best estimates of non-Russians have been that not more than a few thousand political prisoners now are held in camps. The improvement in camp conditions, which he notes may be related to the fiftieth anniversary – major state holidays and anniversaries sometimes produce changes for the better in Soviet prison regions – possibly reflects the continuing publicity which camp regimes have received in the foreign press as a result of the Daniel–Sinyavsky case.

Rumours circulated widely on the eve of the fiftieth anniversary of the Bolshevik revolution that a general amnesty would be declared for all political and literary prisoners, including Yuli Daniel and Andrei Sinyavsky. However, when 7 November 1967 came, the announced amnesty affected only petty criminals. No political persons were released from camp. Sakharov blames this on a struggle between 'rightists' or neo-Stalinists and liberals in the Soviet leadership. His judgement is probably accurate. This struggle was obviously in progress during the months before the fiftieth anniversary and still had not been resolved in 1968.

28. A series of Soviet criminal prosecutions has stemmed from the Daniel–Sinyavsky case and the agitation stimulated by that trial. Aleksandr Ginzburg, a young poet, Yuri Galanskov, also a poet and editor of an avant-garde

dissident mimeographed journal called *Phoenix 1966*, Aleksei Dobrovolsky, a twenty-nine-year-old writer, and Vera Lashkova, a correspondence course student, were arrested in January 1967, and charged with having published *Phoenix,* with compiling a 'white book' documenting the 1966 trial of Daniel and Sinyavsky, and with having contacts with N.T.S., the Narodno–Trudovoi Soyuz, an anti-Soviet organization with headquarters in West Germany and close links to the C.I.A.

Although the four were arrested in January 1967, they were not brought to trial for a year. This delay was in violation of Article 97 of the Soviet Code of Criminal Procedure.

Another young Soviet writer, Vladimir I. Bukovsky, organized a protest against the delay in the trial of Ginzburg and Galanskov. Bukovsky and two associates, Vadim Delone and Yevgeny Kushchev, were arrested as they started to unfurl banners on a Moscow street corner, protesting the injustice of the Ginzburg–Galanskov case. They were arrested by Soviet security agents and sentenced to three years in prison in August 1967.

Sakharov and other Soviet intellectuals interested themselves in the Ginzburg–Galanskov case, protesting the violation of Soviet legalities. As Sakharov notes, he himself wrote to the Central Committee of the Communist Party on 11 February 1967, asking for action in the case. He received no reply and, later on, Dobrovolsky, one of the four defendants turned state's evidence and attempted to involve Sakharov. Dobrovolsky testified in a pretrial investigation that there existed 'a single anti-Communist front ranging from Academicians Sakharov and Leontovich to S.M.O.G.' (an extralegal group of young university writers and artists). Academician Mikhail A. Leontovich, a friend of Sakharov's, was one of the signers with him of the petition of the twenty-five, which was sent to the Central Committee of the Communist party in 1966, warning against rehabilitation of Stalin.

Sakharov blames Vladimir Y. Semichastny for the attempt to involve him in a 'single anti-Communist front'. Semichastny was head of the Soviet K.G.B. or secret police from 1961 until relieved of his post in May 1967. He took over the police job after having served as head of the Komsomols of Communist Youth organization. His predecessor as Komsomol head and K.G.B. chief was Aleksandr Shelepin, youngest member of the Soviet Politburo, a man who has been frequently identified as leader of the faction of neo-Stalinists, a powerful bloc of party figures closely related to the Youth and Police organizations. Beginning with the downfall of Semichastny in the spring of 1967, the members of this bloc have systematically been removed from positions of importance. Shelepin remains in the Politburo but has been removed from the Party Secretariat and placed in charge of Soviet Trade Unions, a downgrading in power and prestige. Despite the weakening of the Police-Youth cabal, there has been no lessening of police pressure on the literary and creative Soviet milieu.

The trial of Ginzburg–Galanskov attracted a remarkable group of protesters, including Pavel M. Litvinov, grandson of the famous Soviet foreign minister, a physicist. Litvinov lost his teaching post in the Moscow Institute of Precision Chemical Technology. Another protester, Mrs Lyudmila I. Ginzburg, mother of Aleksandr Ginzburg, was called to the Secret Police headquarters with her son's fiancée, Irina Zholkovskaya, and warned that if they continued to protest they would be prosecuted under Article 190, Section 1, of the criminal code, providing up to three years' imprisonment on charges of spreading fabrications damaging to the Soviet Union.

General Grigorenko was repeatedly warned by the K.G.B. to cease and desist from efforts on behalf of the defendants. Pavel I. Yakir, a historian and the son of General Iona E. Yakir who was shot by Stalin in a 1937 purge, was warned that the police regarded him as the chief source of dissident activity in Moscow. But he apparently did not lose his job. Aleksandr S. Yesenin-Volpin, mathematics instructor and son of Sergei A. Yesenin, a poet who committed suicide in 1925, was recommitted to a mental institution (he had earlier been committed after publishing in the West modernistic verse critical of the regime). Others who protested against the case included Konstantin Paustovsky, the seventy-five-year-old author who has since died, Pavel Antokolsky, a well-known poet, Veniamin Kaverin, a distinguished author, Vasily Aksyonov, one of the leading young authors, Dr Zamira Asanova, a leading Crimea Tatar, Aleksei Katerin, a writer, Viktor Krazin, an economist, Ilya Gabai, a teacher, Boris Shragin, a philosopher, Anatoly Velitin, a religious writer, Yuli Kim, a teacher, and Yuri Glazov, a linguist. In every case the police or other Soviet agencies brought pressure against the individuals, threatening or insinuating the ill consequences which would ensue if they continued their dissent.

29. The strain of anti-Semitism in Soviet policy and practice never seems to disappear. Russia was the most anti-Semitic of nations before the Bolshevik Revolution. Anti-Semitism as state policy vanished in the early Soviet years. It was reintroduced by Stalin in the 1930s, in part because of his personal prejudices, in part because, as it transpired, many of his enemies among the old Bolsheviks were Jews. He carried out a vicious purge of Jewish cultural institutions in the late 1930s but relaxed during World War II when he felt it necessary to rally Russian and world Jewry to his side. (Yet, in 1941 anti-Semitism was openly employed as state and party policy at the time of the Battle of Moscow and for two years thereafter.) After World War II, Stalin became more and more anti-Semitic, personally and in policy. His last years were marked by enormous secret anti-Semitic purges and so-called 'plots' which had Jews as their focal target.

Stalin's use of anti-Semitism as a state policy was repudiated by his successors. They halted open discrimination against Jews in government and education and brought to an end the purge of Jews from Soviet institutions, their exile to Siberia, and their execution on a variety of charges. However, Khrushchev himself was almost openly anti-Semitic, largely, it would seem, due to prejudices acquired during his youth in the endemically anti-Semitic Ukraine. A strain of anti-Semitism has been continued to this day in the Soviet Union, manifesting itself in part by violent hostility towards the Jewish church, Jewish communities, Zionism, and, often, against Jewish cultural heritages. Discrimination against Jews in important state and party posts continues. No Jews hold positions in the Politburo and there is only one in the highest organs of government. There are no Jews in the high command of the Soviet Armed Forces, or in top echelons of Soviet diplomacy. No Jews edit important party organs. On the other hand, there are many Jews in key scientific, cultural, and educational institutions. It is barely possible that Sakharov is Jewish.

30. The continuance of restrictions on the Crimean Tatars long after all other Soviet nationalities victimized by Stalin had been rehabilitated and received partial compensation for their sufferings is still unexplained. Sakharov's estimate of the population loss of the Tatars, forty-six per cent, is the first which is known to have been made. It may serve as an indication of the very heavy loss of life which was involved in Stalin's punitive movements of populations. These peoples customarily were bodily shipped, often at a few hours' notice, by locked cattle car for thousands of miles on trips that might continue for months. There was little or no sanitation, only subsistence rations or less, frequent and persistent shortages of water, and no medical attention. The shipments were carried out in the depth of winter in temperatures far below zero or in the blazing mid-summer temperatures of the Soviet Central Asian desert. The victims were often dumped into wilderness areas or regions of pestilence and disease. For example,

among the Volga Germans deported to Tadjikstan, the losses due to malaria and subtropical diseases were estimated at one-third of the evacuees or higher. The losses in populations shipped to the far north, to Yakutia, ran higher.

Only today are thoughtful Great Russians beginning to ponder the extent of nationality problems within the Soviet Union. The Soviet has about seventy major nationalities within its borders and a total of about 160 peoples with identifiable characteristics, languages, and traditions. Many of the nationalities remain disaffected despite fifty years of Soviet life, largely because of repressive and Great Russian chauvinistic policies. Lenin regarded the nationality problem as one of the most critical of the Russian Empire. He and his Bolsheviks liked to call Tsarist Russia the 'prisonhouse of nations' because of the Tsar's repressions of minority peoples. They pledged themselves to redress the situation. In the first days of the Revolution, Lenin offered the minority nations the freedom to disassociate themselves from Russia, should they desire. When Finland declared her independence, Lenin and his associates had second thoughts. However, largely for military reasons, Poland and the Baltic States did obtain independence. In the Caucasus, independent republics were established in Georgia, Armenia, and Azerbaidjan but all were ultimately incorporated into the Union. The independent Ukrainian state was absorbed, as were independent governments of varying political persuasion and stability in Central Asia and the Far East. The right of a Soviet republic to declare its independence of the Union is guaranteed by the Soviet Constitution. But no republic would ever be permitted to exercise this right.

31. Sakharov compares the upsurge of neo-Stalinism in the Soviet Union to the manifestations of McCarthyism in the United States in the early 1950s. This comparison must be understood in Soviet terms. McCarthyism was underevalu-

ated as a political force by the Soviet Union because the Communist propaganda line had so long insisted that the prevailing climate in the United States and the West was dominated by anti-Communist hysteria, anti-Soviet sentiment, and Fascist tendencies. Thus, when McCarthy appeared on the scene, it seemed to the Russian public merely one more manifestation of a continuing tendency rather than a new and striking phenomenon, related to a dramatic upsurge in right-wing antilibertarianism. When Sakharov relates the current neo-Stalinism to McCarthyism, he means a lesser tendency than the American reader might assume. McCarthy was able to persecute and drive from public office a substantial number of prominent officials. He created a nation-wide climate of anti-intellectualism, fear, and suspicion. Up to 1968 the Soviet scene did not match this picture. Rather, the neo-Stalinists tended to confine themselves to small targets (students, obscure writers, etc), and their repressions evoked a powerful and remarkable display of public opposition by important public figures in Russia. Sakharov himself is an example of this. It should be noted that when Stalin embarked upon his long career of terror, there was no similar outpouring of public indignation, no poets standing up and warning against his acts; no scientists composing long manifestos. Already Stalin's climate of terror and suppression was too intense.

32. At no point in his manifesto does Sakharov find himself more at odds with the Soviet government than in his views on Czechoslovakia. He sees the Czechs as embarking on an initiative which carries the hopes of the future of socialism (that is, liberal communism) and the future of mankind. He calls for Soviet political support of Czechoslovakia and increased economic aid for the Czechs.

Soviet policy on Czechoslovakia took the directly opposite tack. The Russians attempted by political, military, psychological, and economic pressure to compel the Czechs to turn the clock back, to end the political liberalization, to restore the Novotny forces to power, to toe the line of Communist orthodoxy. Moscow demonstrated its willingness to risk war and engage in armed intervention, to prevent the spread of the 'Czech disease' elsewhere within the Communist world.

The contrast between the views of Sakharov and his government on Czechoslovakia reflects the deep schism within Russia over the dramatic liberalization undertaken by Czechoslovakia. Broad segments of the Soviet intelligentsia side with Sakharov and against government policy on this question. The fact that in spite of these views Moscow decided to impose the utmost pressure on Prague reflects the fears of the Soviet military and the conservatives in the government over the consequences of Prague's new path. The military feared that it inevitably would lead to a breach in the Warsaw pact. Their reaction is like that of militarists anywhere. Any move is justified to preserve their defence structure. The Moscow conservatives feared Prague for another and graver reason. They believed that if Prague succeeded in liberalizing its regime, in ending the censorship, in permitting freedom of speech, freedom of the press, freedom for competing political parties, and ultimately free elections, the demand for similar liberties would become irresistible in Russia. It is probable that they are right. The Sakharov manifesto is itself evidence of the depth and breadth of sentiment about liberalization.

33. Sakharov's ski-race figure of speech, in which he sees the United States and the Soviet Union as two skiers of equal strength racing downhill with the United States ahead, breaking the snow, and the Soviet Union following along, more easily, in the American path, provides a dramatic and realistic analogy to the actual course of technological and economic development of the two countries. It implies (as Sakharov recognizes) that there is little or no chance for any early Soviet victory, for the attainment of Khrushchev's goals of 'catching up and surpassing' the

United States, for the reaching of the statistical levels set by Khrushchev in his blueprint for the Communist future. Khrushchev's blueprint was drafted in 1961. In it he forecast that Russia would exceed the United States in many key areas by 1970 and race ahead to a substantial lead by 1980. Sakharov accurately notes the unrealism of such a prognosis.

He goes further than this to point out the vitality which the capitalist system, and particularly the American system, has demonstrated. It was Marx's prediction (as well as that of Lenin and Stalin) that capitalism was headed for inevitable downfall because of its internal contradictions – particularly the intensification of the struggle by employers to enslave and impoverish the working class and on the part of the working class to take an increasing share of the profits.

Sakharov recognizes that the working class of the West, far from being impoverished by advanced capitalism, is benefiting richly and that there are no signs that capitalism is on the verge of collapse.

He offers the reasonable suggestion that both socialism, as the Soviet calls its economy, and capitalism have shown vitality and an ability to improve the living standards of their people. He believes in the 'convergence' theory which has been propounded by western theorists, both socialist and non-socialist, under which the societies of Russia and the United States seem to be borrowing valuable features from each other, thus leading in the long run to the creation of systems which are more and more compatible and which do not carry inevitable seeds of military collision and fatal war.

To the criticism that he has embraced 'revisionist' or non-Marxist positions, Sakharov offers the reasonable rejoinder that one reason why Western economies have proved successful is that they have incorporated socialist principles into their systems.

34. Sakharov offers an unusual and ingenious argument

against an American revolution – that it would be contrary to the interests of the working class. He estimates that the well-to-do in the United States absorb no more than twenty per cent of the national production (he probably over-estimates) and that this is somewhat less than the normal increase in production over a five-year period. Since a revolution would, at a minimum, halt economic development for at least five years and probably more, he does not see it in the interest of the American proletariat to indulge in such a violent exercise.

He is at pains to distinguish his argument from one which might be applied against the Bolshevik revolution. This is a famous remark made in a letter by Friedrich Engels to the Russian revolutionary Vera Zasulich. She had written to Engels in 1885, shortly after the death of Marx, asking his opinion of a book by the Russian Marxian theorist Plekanov. In his reply, he suggested that Russia was approaching a revolutionary situation and added that it did not make a great deal of difference who brought the revolution about because the people who made the revolution would be swept away by the explosion.

'The people who boasted that they had made a revolution have always seen the next day that they had no idea what they were doing, that the revolution made did not in the least resemble the one they would have liked to make,' he wrote. 'That is what Hegel calls the irony of history, an irony which few historic personalities escape.'

Engels wrote, of course, thirty-two years before the Bolshevik Revolution and nearly fifty years before Stalin shackled his terrible power on the Soviet state. But, as Sakharov notes, his words eloquently apply to what happened in the Soviet Union.

He sees no reason for such an event in the United States nor in other advanced western countries. Nor, he points out, do Communists in those countries themselves.

35. Sakharov's comparison between the income levels and

standard of living in the Soviet Union and the United States is fairly accurate according to the calculations of American economists, although his estimate of forty per cent of the Soviet population suffering economic straits sounds high. The five per cent of Soviet population in the top managerial group commands an income in comparative Soviet terms which is as much higher than the ordinary Soviet working man's as that of the American counterpart group. However, in absolute terms the American managerial class earns higher annual salaries than the Soviet managers. The Soviet managers obtain much of their advantage from special privileges – automobiles, chauffeurs, better living quarters, privileged status for themselves and their families which are not available at any price to ordinary working men and women.

Sakharov reveals an often-suspected but not heretofore confirmed secret of the Stalin days – that managers got a concealed bonus in the form of a kind of kickback from their employer, the state. This was the pay in 'sealed envelopes' which did not show on the factory books and was in addition to their substantial salaries and bonuses for cutting costs and increasing profits to the state.

More important than these monetary awards, however, were the special opportunities introduced by Stalin and continued to this day – the ability to get scarce consumer goods, TV sets, automobiles, household furnishings, high quality clothing, through under-the-counter arrangements with the retail trade system or through 'closed' stores or buying arrangements which only high officials and managers shared.

36. Sakharov's proposals for a revision of the Soviet system of prices, markets, investment priority, utilization of economic resources, production stimulants, and the introduction of market factors echoes the demands of Soviet economists for radical revision of the Soviet economic system to give it the vitality of the free market economy of the West.

Almost all the Communist countries of eastern Europe are experimenting with schemes of 'market socialism'. In the Soviet Union itself, the introduction of the so-called Liberman system has brought a widespread change in factory management. Under the Liberman plan, factories compete on a cost-and-profit basis, pricing their goods to the market and competing against each other for orders. About half of Soviet industrial enterprises are now on the Liberman system. It does not wholly remove the dictatorial powers of the State Plan managers. But it restricts them and encourages individual enterprise.

37. The accounts of Theodore Sorensen and Arthur Schlesinger, Jr, about the Kennedy–Khrushchev confrontation in Vienna do not entirely support Sakharov's version of President Kennedy's appeal to Khrushchev not to press demands which Kennedy could not meet without courting defeat in the elections. However, Kennedy did forcefully advance the thesis that in the interest of Soviet-American relations he trusted that Mr Khrushchev would not force a crisis over so delicate and dangerous a subject as Berlin. It would have been consistent with Mr Kennedy's frankness if he had pointed out to the Soviet Chairman the political implications of such a crisis and the limits of practical political action on his part. Khrushchev did take a tough line with President Kennedy and may have exaggerated the President's remarks in briefing his associates in Moscow on the nature of the Vienna discussions.

Afterword

By Harrison E. Salisbury

THE WORLD IN THE YEAR 2000

PROBABLY no calendar event in man's existence possesses the evocative quality of the millennia. The thousand-year span of life, the thousand-year anniversary captures mankind's imagination in a way nothing else does.

We now stand on the threshold of such a watermark — the year 2000.

What can we anticipate in the epoch which lies just ahead?

Possibly because of the cynicism of the age, possibly because we remember too well the unfulfilled predictions made for the twentieth century, possibly because two great World Wars have left a residue of pragmatism, hedonism, a tendency to live for today and let the morrow take care of itself, there is in the western world a notable absence of utopian dreams of what lies ahead.

We are so accustomed to thinking of ourselves as a 'free' society and Russia and the Communist world as a 'closed' system that it comes as a shock and a surprise to find a man born, raised, and living his entire life under the red banner of Communism, who is, indeed, somewhat younger than the Soviet regime itself, setting forth not some visionary concept under which the year 2000 will witness the final and total victory for Communism but an intensely realistic forecast of a unitary world society in which, by modification and interchange, Communism and Capitalism discover a means of living together in peace and goodwill with each other and with the turbulent and murky forces now emerging from the backward lands of Asia and Africa and from the ghettos of America itself.

The central concept evolved by Andrei Sakharov is that

131

the world can survive *only* if the United States and the Soviet Union establish a means for living without war within a cooperative framework in which they jointly resolve the problems which lie beyond the immediate threat of nuclear disaster.

For the sake of simplicity he has divided the remaining years of the twentieth century into four roughly equal but overlapping periods. The first period (almost half over already) of 1960–80 would be essentially occupied with the evolution of a new socio-political system in the Communist world – the rise of a multi-party system or of competing programmes and viewpoints, freely manifest within Communist parties.

The democratization of the Communist regimes would not wipe away the economic basis of these countries. The Communist economic system, government ownership of the means of production, government direction of national economy, the ban on the private ownership of the means of production would continue. But the political basis of the Communist states would change. The dictatorship by a single party and of the single party by a single leader or oligarchy would end with the flourishing of divergent and competing opinions.

During this phase the ideological split and warfare between what Sakharov might call the 'free' Communist states and the closed pseudo-Communist state of China would intensify. The conflict would deepen and he does not preclude the possibility of armed intervention in China by United Nations forces in order to establish freedom of human rights for the Chinese peoples.

The second period, occupying the years 1972–85, would be devoted to the establishment of a firm basis of permanent coexistence on a peaceful basis between the United States and other capitalist states, on the one hand, and the Socialist or Communist world on the other. He believes that there will be sufficient transformation of each society so that the convergence theory will be the dominating factor. As western society becomes more socialized and the Communist world more democratized he sees the stage set for both societies to join in a concerted effort to overwhelm the forces of racism and militarism which will still persist in the world.

The crusade for abolition of racism and of militarism would be carried forward by Capitalism and Communist states under the flag of the United Nations although by this time the concepts of 'Communism' and 'Capitalism' as differing social orders will have become largely meaningless.

Only in the third stage would the United States and the Soviet Union turn the torrent of their resources towards lifting up to western standards the poorer nations of the world. In these years (1972–90) they would begin to devote twenty per cent of their national incomes to creating massive fertilizer and irrigation works employing nuclear power in an attack upon the critical underproduction of food. They would join in a global effort to exploit the full resources of the sea for food and chemical reserves. Great plants would be built for synthesizing fats, proteins, and carbohydrates. The developed nations would open the throttle of their agricultural and industrial production to produce for the use of underdeveloped nations to the full extent of their capabilities.

It is this titanic task which Sakharov believes might halt or slow down the economic growth of the United States (and the Soviet Union). In reality it would undoubtedly lead to the most intensive and explosive economic growth the world has ever seen. It is, of course, feasible only in a society in which arms and military production have been cut to minimum levels.

The final stage would see the establishment of a world government on a basis of 'socialist convergence', harnessing the matchless and still hardly envisaged sources of nuclear power from the utilization of uranium, thorium, deuterium, and lithium.

The expansion of population and the command of new nuclear and technological resources will impel large numbers of persons to live on extraplanetary locales – other planets, the moon, satellites, asteroids.

Full control of life processes, including those involved in reproduction and death, will place in man's hands the capability for controlling both his environment and his own personality.

As the alternative to a system of world government, led by the United States and the Soviet Union, dedicated to the positive and rational control of the scientific-technological miracles which lie just ahead, Sakharov envisages a world quickly descending into chaos and, in all probability, total nuclear destruction.

The forces which man now controls are so pervasive, their potential so cataclysmic that without the broadest-scale collaboration and utilization of man's capacity for social management he inevitably will destroy himself. Sakharov's view of the brink on which mankind stands is one shared by most thoughtful scientists of the western world – a belief that our potential for destruction has grown so radically that the odds upon the world arriving at the year 2000 may be stated in the negative.

A physicist who has participated in the unleashing of the most destructive force known to man – the hydrogen bomb – is hardly likely to close his eyes to the spectre which his intellect has brought to mankind. What may surprise Americans is the fact that a Soviet physicist should construct a vision of the future which draws so eclectically not merely from the materials of the Marxist world in which he has always lived but from the total human experience. Sakharov's blueprint is constructed not from elements of hostility to the non-Communist world but with a universalism which sees both the flaws in his own society and the positive virtues (as well as the terrible shortfalls) of that society with which the Soviet has been so long (and often unnaturally) at conflict.

Afterword

The American surprise at Sakharov's imagination is compounded in part of American ignorance of the reality of the Soviet intelligentsia and the Russian milieu. For nearly a hundred and fifty years Russian men and women have looked at the life which their country has led and the nations beyond their frontiers with humanist eyes, strongly shaded with idealist inclinations. The Revolution of 1917 was a product of those dreams of a better world, of the warmest utopian aspirations. As George F. Kennan has so wisely observed, the Russian Revolution was the product of one hundred years of Russian striving towards western liberal objectives. It is a bleak fact that, almost by a whim of fate, or as Hegel would call it, 'the irony of history', the revolution made under the banner of the purest morals and the noblest of aims has been perverted into a paranoid nightmare. But, the perversion of the Revolution has served to reinforce the striving of the Russian intelligentsia to recapture the original dream. The Bolsheviks with their iron discipline, their doctrinaire immobility, their susceptibility to aberrational oligarchy may, from the vantage point of the year 2000, be seen as only a temporary job in the long Russian surge to enter the liberal democratic society which arose in the eighteenth century in western Europe and America.

It is not too much to suggest that, having survived the Golgotha of Stalin's prison state, Russia – if it escapes the dead hand of the neo-Stalinists – could take the lead as regards freedom of intellect, freedom of conscience, freedom of the human will – the cause for which so many of her countrymen gave their lives. It is fashionable to compare the Soviet regime unfavourably with the mobility of person and of thought which is common in the West. But it is not impossible that the nation which was the first to put a man into orbit outside the earth may soon permit its citizens to choose their own orbits.

Sakharov is not the Kremlin. His views stand in the sharpest contrast to the conventional, bureaucratic, unimaginative, and more than slightly repressive policies of the Kosygin-Brezhnev regime. Yet, the potential for change and modification even within present Soviet terms should not be underestimated.

Russia may still harass its poets; may imprison dissident minor writers; may threaten its most gifted creators with the direst of fates, as in the case of Solzhenitsyn. Yet Russia and America have demonstrated in the past few years more signs of maturity than of regression into the dangerous confrontations of the Dulles epoch. Vietnam has not been permitted to deteriorate into a new 'cold war'. There has been genuine progress towards the control of those weapons which threaten the world with destruction. But, if both Moscow and Washington have been impelled towards greater sanity by worries over China, then the Czech crisis and all the dangerous symptoms of Muscovite regression pose new obstacles toward political détente.

The problems which overhang the world have never been more dangerous. If we escape nuclear suicide we may drown in a sea of humanity; suffocate in a poison-filled atmosphere; succumb to pollution of the seas and despoliation of the land; descend into robotry with the aid of chemicals and electrodes or perish at the edict of a nonhuman computer.

But at the most perilous of moments we hear a voice from a most unlikely source. Out of Moscow comes a manifesto, a call for action, an architectural plan for the future, an analysis of human forces which compensates both for frailty and for creativity, a nondogmatic approach to the gravest of problems.

Sakharov has drafted his presentation not in terms of absolutes but as a vehicle for discussion. It has been laid before Soviet society for advice, comment, and criticism. Now it is presented to American readers in the same spirit. It is not dicta. It is designed to stimulate.

There is roughly a quarter century left before the year 2000. Sakharov does not claim universality for his thoughts. But he would agree that unless his blueprint – or some reasonable variation – is adopted by the principal societies of the world, the prospects of survival into the second millennium are virtually nil.

MORE ABOUT PENGUINS
AND PELICANS

Penguinews, which appears every month, contains details of all the new books issued by Penguins as they are published. From time to time it is supplemented by *Penguins in Print*, which is a complete list of all titles available. (There are some five thousand of these.)

A specimen copy of *Penguinews* will be sent to you free on request. For a year's issues (including the complete lists) please send £1·00 if you live in the British Isles, or if you live elsewhere. Just write to Dept EP, Penguin Books Ltd, Harmondsworth, Middlesex, enclosing a cheque or postal order, and your name will be added to the mailing list.

In the U.S.A.: For a complete list of books available from Penguin in the United States write to Dept CS, Penguin Books Inc., 7110 Ambassador Road, Baltimore, Maryland 21207.

In Canada: For a complete list of books available from Penguin in Canada write to Penguin Books Canada Ltd, 41 Steelcase Road West, Markham, Ontario.

SCIENCE IN HISTORY

J. D. Bernal

'This stupendous work ... is a magnificent synoptic view of the rise of science and its impact on society which leaves the reader awe-struck by Professor Bernal's encyclopedic knowledge and historical sweep' – *The Times Literary Supplement*.

Until recently many scientists, concerned with the overriding importance of current knowledge, would have agreed with Henry Ford that 'History is bunk'. Patently, however, science has influenced society, just as society has influenced science ... and progress will be quicker and surer if the lessons of the past have been well read.

J. D. Bernal's monumental work, *Science in History*, was the first full-scale attempt to analyse the reciprocal relations of science and society throughout history, from the perfection of the flint hand-axe to the hydrogen bomb. In this remarkable study he illustrates the impetus given to (and the limitations placed upon) discovery and invention by pastoral, agricultural, feudal, capitalist, and socialist systems, and conversely the ways in which science has altered economic, social, and political beliefs and practices.

The whole work has been lavishly illustrated for this Pelican edition and is now offered to a wider public in four volumes.

NOT FOR SALE IN THE U.S.A.

MY TESTIMONY

Anatoly Marchenko

The first detailed report on Soviet prison camps as they are today.

'An extraordinarily important book . . . Perhaps not since Dostoyevsky's *House of the Dead* has there been such a totally realistic, detailed, factual and yet profoundly compassionate and human account of Russian prison and camp life . . . *My Testimony* is a searchlight cutting through the murk of the real Russia' – *Daily Telegraph*

'It is a book that must be read by anyone who cares to know about contemporary Russia . . . compulsive reading' – *Guardian*

'This amazing book . . . The emotions of the men of Vladimir and Mordovia are portrayed sensitively and accurately. Marchenko has in common with Solzhenitsyn a trait of dropping telling details in a deadpan way . . . His testimony is a stark, impressive work, written by a very courageous and honest man. He has told the truth and sacrificed himself for that truth with the same finality as if he had soaked himself with petrol and put a match to it. He is all the braver for having done this consciously, knowing where he was and what would be the consequences . . .' – Gerald Brooke in the *Sunday Telegraph*

RED SQUARE AT NOON

Natalia Gorbanevskaya

On 21 August 1968 Soviet troops and their allies invaded Czechoslovakia. Four days later eight young people were arrested after demonstrating peacefully in Moscow's Red Square against the invasion.

After the trial Natalia Gorbanevskaya courageously used her 'freedom' to compile this factual account of exactly what happened in Moscow on and after 15 August 1968.

Now she too is permanently confined in a 'special psychiatric hospital'.

Such is the price of raising a banner of protest against Soviet imperialism in the Red Square.

NOT FOR SALE IN THE U.S.A.

TWENTY LETTERS TO A FRIEND

Svetlana Alliluyeva

Svetlana Alliluyeva, daughter of Stalin, was at the centre of some of the most violent upheavals of the twentieth century.

Her account of the period – a time when most records were falsified or destroyed – is simple, true, and unique.

Twenty Letters to a Friend is more than a vivid footnote to a reign of terror. It is an astonishing, moving, personal document . . . the literary event of our generation.

'A unique masterpiece . . . all past histories of Russia will have to be re-written in the light of this book' – Edward Crankshaw in the *Observer*